Chef Kimberly's answer to the question
"Where are the Female and Minority Chefs?"

HERE I AM!

Chef Kimberly Brock Brown,
CEPC, CCA, ACE, AAC

authorHOUSE®

AuthorHouse™
1663 Liberty Drive
Bloomington, IN 47403
www.authorhouse.com
Phone: 1-800-839-8640

Published by AuthorHouse 10/23/2012

ISBN: 978-1-4772-7298-5 (sc)
ISBN: 978-1-4772-7296-1 (hc)
ISBN: 978-1-4772-7297-8 (e)

Library of Congress Control Number: 2012917662

Any people depicted in stock imagery provided by Thinkstock are models, and such images are being used for illustrative purposes only. Certain stock imagery © Thinkstock.

This book is printed on acid-free paper.

Acknowledgements

To God be the Glory for the things He has allowed me to see, do and have. For using me and my life experiences to be a Blessing to others as they endeavor to reach their goals and fulfill their destiny.

Thanks Mom & my dearly departed Dad, Cheryl Dixon, Judy Brock-Mack & Paul Brock for the life, love and support given through these years. I am who I am in part because of you.

Bianca and Brock Brown, two of the reasons why I do what I do and what keeps me going and grounded. Mom loves you dearly.

My aunts (Lovia & Marie-RIP,) Bessie & Adrienne, cousins, niece & nephew, sister friends Eliese Allen, Dominique Milton, Naomi Sampson, Jakki Jefferson, Barbra Johnson, Garcia Williams, Marcia Drummond, who have prayed for and with me, shed tears of joy and pain, and gave words of encouragement through the years, I love you. I thank you.

For the fellows who stepped up when I needed a hand or additional support and another point of view. Bill Mack, John Orr and Samuel Deveaux I thank you for the wisdom and strength you offered.

Steve McLeod-Bryant, the support and friendship over these years from you and my dear friend, your wife Aleta (may she forever RIP) and the rest of the family has been phenomenal! Thank you seems woefully inadequate so I'll just say a friendly 6 No!

My colleagues and friends who I admire and look up to; Dennie Veasey CEC,CCA, Shacafrica Simmons, Natasha Capper CEPC, Henry Douglas CEC,AAC, Herman Packer CEC,AAC, Clayton Sherrod, John Kacala CEC,AAC, Robert Stegall-Smith CEC,AAC, Charlie Mattocks CEC, CCA, AAC, Tom Young(RIP), Louis

Perrotte CEC, AAC Reimund Pitz, CEC, CCE, AAC, Marvin Woods, Scott Barton, Jaime Aquilar, and all who have given me culinary inspiration and words of support and encouragement, in this crazy culinary world that we love so much.

To my associates who have helped me with inspiration, encouragement and their talents. Thank you Danielle Gillard for your writing and mad computer skills! Who said the younger generation is lost?! Holly Stucker for your keen eye and sense of humor which kept me smiling.

The ABC Low Country Live Family-Ericka Zapecza, Laura Harris, Dave Williams, Jon Bruce, Amy Kehm, camera crew and Ms Yvonne who's angelic voice is music to my ears. Thank you for the opportunity and for treating me so graciously.

Last but not at all in the least, my business development manager, driver, partner and friend Lee H. Moultrie II. Thank you for the vision and ability to get the job done! For pushing when I needed it and for not giving up when the going got rough and I couldn't see past the next day. "Discovery consists of seeing what everybody has seen and thinking what nobody has thought"-Albert Szent-Gyorgyi. God Bless you for embracing this sentiment and putting into fruition the plan.

Preface

We all have a purpose. We may not know it at the beginning, but we're here for a reason; and our journey, our path, is to find the reasons why we're here for that moment, for that minute, for that second in time to be the light for somebody else, to share the light with somebody else, and to have that light shine on you. Are you inspiring someone today or yesterday or maybe the day before that?

I believe that our parents, our upbringing, and our environment make us what we are today. If you didn't grow up with your parents, or if you grew up with abusive parents, or if you grew up with parents who didn't love or treat you the way you wanted to be loved, your behaviors today are magnified by what you perceived to be a loss growing up. There is no easy way to say this, but get over it. You have choices to make. You can choose to do better. You can choose to have better. You can choose to be who you want to be. So, if you want to be the "woe is me, I'm the child nobody loved, I'm the child who Mommy didn't care for, I'm the child who didn't do this, didn't have that, didn't get that," or you can be the child, "Yeah, I had it rough growing up, but I've learned to blossom and thrive, and grow, and learn, and lean on people and others for support." Those life lessons start early.

So, what doesn't kill you makes you stronger. As the third child of Ellen and Clifton, what didn't kill me made me stronger. Seeing how one sister would stand up to the other sister and what was her perception of what was right versus what was wrong, left a mark on me. Do you stand up? Do you stick up for the person, for the thing, or for a cause when you believe something is wrong? It's too easy not to.

There was a saying that was drilled into my head back when I was in grade school, "If it is to be, it is up to me." I'm thankful that of all the churches that we visited growing up, and there were many, that my mom settled on the one that still holds the foundation of what I believe and live my life by today. The power of positive thinking is a beautiful thing. It's what I tend to lean towards, that there's always, always room in that glass for more. It's not half-empty, it's half-full. I am that I am. I am all that I can be. If it is to be, it is up to me. Who knew that this little girl of Ellen and Clifton Brock would be here today as a Certified Executive Pastry Chef, the first African-American female inducted into the honor society of the American Academy of Chefs of the American Culinary Federation, talking to you, writing a book, making it happen? Who knew? I couldn't have told you that. But, things click. Things happen. God has a way of putting people in your life, putting obstacles in your way. I agree with the saying: don't move the mountain, just give me the strength to climb. Don't pray for patience because you'll get it. So, I pray for the strength to climb, the strength to succeed, the strength to endure, to have a purpose, to give somebody else a purpose, to be that little light that shines. If I can help someone, then let it begin with me.

There have been principle ingredients within me that have influenced the choices I have made that bring me to where I am today, and they are the same principle ingredients that I will use to help me continue on into my future. The stories in the pages that follow describe the mountains I've climbed and the challenges I've endured and succeeded in on the way to finding and fulfilling my purpose. There are no excuses here. I am one female, Afro-American Executive Chef, seeking to record the unique recipe of my life in hopes that you can find something within my story to inspire you to take ownership of the principle ingredients in your life. So when the conversation comes your way about where are all of the women Chefs? Why are there no minority Chefs in charge of restaurants, country clubs and other establishments? This will empower you to make claim so that you can stand right along beside me and boldly say with me, "Here I Am."

CHAPTER 1

Equipping the Cooking Space

A recipe may only be as good as its ingredients, but a Chef is defined by how innovative they are in using the raw materials around them to create dishes that are more appealing to both the eyes and the palette than the average person can imagine. This means that a Chef has to be able to look at the materials that are made available to them and use their past experiences and learned techniques to combine ingredients to make them better than they were on their own. When you think about it, life works the same way. It doesn't really matter how perfect things were for you growing up, or even how much you liked it. It's all about what you choose to do with it.

Who knew that a little girl who grew up in the western suburbs of Chicago would become a Chef? My parents were middle class working people. My father mostly worked two factory/manufacturing jobs and Mom worked a 9 to 5 office job. With a house to maintain and four kids to feed, I am sure the budget was tight, especially after they divorced while I was in elementary school. But when I think back, I don't remember ever thinking about us as a struggling family. Well, I remember some struggles, but they were not financial, most of my struggles dealt with being a middle child making her own way in the world.

We lived about 15 miles west of downtown Chicago in a suburb called Maywood. I loved hearing the different dialects and the different languages people spoke. I could go on this block and get this kind of cuisine from this country and go just two doors down and get a different kind of cuisine from another country. It really is a melting pot, or a mixed salad, in that everybody is different but working together for the good of the community. For the most part, you get along and it's just a nice large scale blended community, and there's always something to do.

My family and I lived in this big old two story house with big bay windows that sat on a corner lot. I remember it well because one of the bay windows was attached to the bedroom I shared with my sister Judy. I loved the three-window view! We had this big backyard, a big side yard, and a good sized front yard. Cheryl is seven years older than me and always had her own room. Paul is two years younger than me and always had his own room because he was the only boy. So that left Judy, who is two years older than me, to share a room while we were growing up.

Naturally, all of our relationships are a little different with each other. Judy and I have always shared pretty much everything. Not only did we share a room with bunk beds, we shared dreams. She slept on the top bunk because I preferred the bottom bunk. I had too much fun kicking the mattress up in and air while she was trying to sleep. Why would I give up the bottom bunk? I remember that she and I would always have little games that we played. Like the last one in bed would always have to cut the light off. We would try to trip each other up so that we could make it into bed first! We have always been close too, but we did have our differences. Our room looked like it belonged to Felix and Oscar from the Odd Couple. You knew what belonged to Felix and you knew what was Oscar's. Judy's side was always cleaned up and mine was a little more, well, let's just say, "disheveled." That's why I know to check under my kid's beds when I tell them to clean their room. They are just like their mother so I know exactly what they're doing!

My oldest sister Cheryl, was always into something totally different from what Judy and I usually got into. When she was getting into boys and wanting to go to the little parties at the local rec' center and go roller skating and be more social, my sister Judy was more of a bookworm, and still is, and would rather be in the house studying, reading a book, or at the library. As a matter of fact, Judy ended up getting a part-time job at the library. Often people tried to compare me to her because we are close in age, asking me why I don't read a lot like she does and why I'm not valedictorian like her. My answer was that she had that covered for the whole family and there was no need for me to go that route too! I always floated between the two of them. And when my brother, Paul, came along two years after me, you could just sit him in front of a TV and he would be good to go. Sometimes I would sit there and veg out on some cartoons with him too. Sometimes we'd play with the little matchbox cars; I liked to take my Barbie dolls for a joy ride. We got along well too. He did pretty well to survive in a household full of women.

Let me say right off that we, the children of Clifton and Ellen, were always grateful that our mother got the family cooking gene. Between her two sisters, our mom was hands down the better cook! My mom had us in the kitchen daily. We were always chopping, stirring, grinding, basting, and washing pots and pans and dishes. Mom was known for making a fabulous caramel cake and cat head rolls. There were always requests for her caramel cake during the Holiday season. It brought sheer delight upon arrival. It was the centerpiece of the dessert table and the first item to run out. The cat heads were flakey, soft, yeast rolls of goodness that made the whole house smell like the Bernie Brothers Bakery. There is something to be said for the smell of fresh bread baking in your kitchen. Mom had to really watch those rolls or there would be none for the meal!

My dad knew his way around the kitchen too. He taught me how to prepare one of his favorite breakfasts-two eggs over real easy, toast, bacon, American fried potatoes and coffee. It's not like he sat me down and taught me how to make it all in one day, the lessons were spread out over time. See, my mom was a coffee drinker, so we would make coffee all the time. Whether it was in the morning or while she was sitting in her recliner later that night, it was not unusual to hear, "Will you make me a cup of coffee?" American fried potatoes, or skillet potatoes, or even home fried potatoes, whatever you want to call them, were a staple in our household. On Saturday and Sunday, potatoes were going in that skillet and we were going to get down with potatoes, some eggs, salt pork or country sausage or bacon. We were going to make it happen. Because my father usually worked two jobs he was rarely home in the mornings for breakfast. And even if he was home, he was usually asleep. So if there was a morning when Daddy surprised us to join us for breakfast, we made sure that he got his favorite-two eggs over real easy, toast, bacon, American fried potatoes and coffee.

For me, my brother and my sisters, cooking was what we grew up with. It was our chore. Somebody was always cooking something, every day. At times we went out to eat too, but somebody was always in the kitchen cooking. It was either your turn to wash the dishes or it was your turn to cook or your turn to clean the house. Even if we had to pull up a chair to the sink, we were going to bust some suds. Our chores usually rotated weekly, but if you were on punishment you would get two weeks. Mom made sure that our chores were usually age appropriate. When it was your turn to cook, you could use recipes out of a cookbook that was passed down from the oldest to the youngest child, called "My First Cookbook." I think I still have that book in my well-traveled dorm trunk. It taught you how to measure and how to do all the cooking basics while being age appropriate.

We were all able and capable of cooking and there was always food in the house. My mom even had a green thumb, and would have us out there weeding between the greens, tomatoes, or whatever else she had out there growing at the time. She must have gotten the green thumb from her hometown, because when she sent us down to her mother, our grandmother, in Missouri there was always somebody giving us food from their farm.

I remember this one time Grandma must have brought home a fifty pound bag of cabbage. All of us sat there cleaning and chopping up cabbage. Oh, my God! It just went on forever! She wanted to make some sauerkraut and can the rest so that she would have some year round. Before we were halfway through I was wishing to never see any more cabbage! We were also used to making a weekend trek to Michigan or Indiana during the summer picking time to harvest on the farms and bring it all back to can and freeze them. We did all that stuff growing up. So we always had blueberries all year round because we canned them and froze them, and we'd be making blueberry pancakes, blueberry sauces, blueberry ice cream, blueberry cobbler… we would do everything. It was not just blueberries either, we would also pick apples to make apple juice and apple butter. I mean, it didn't matter, we were doing it.

I believe it was the look of satisfaction and the joy in which the food was eaten that made me want to cook. What a great feeling of accomplishment to know that for that meal, be it Friday night supper or the family meal on Sunday after church, I gave someone else comfort, satisfaction and good food. The joy of cooking indeed is alive and well in my soul, but as much as I enjoyed cooking and making little cakes and muffins with my Easy-Bake Oven-I liked to eat out too.

Sometimes we would go to a fish market. It used to be a few blocks away from the house. When we went there we would be able to point out a particular victim in the fish tank, "I want that one," and they would catch, kill, clean and fillet it for you right then and there. That would be our catch, or dinner, for the night. I could watch them catching, gutting and filleting for hours. I had no fear about watching that sort of thing because we used to go fishing all the time. I thought I could fillet with the best of them. I did enjoy going to the market and watching them do it for us.

Everyone knows about Chicago's pizza, and I loved those nights that we would have pizza delivered to us. It was always from a local restaurant. There were no Domino's, Papa John's or Pizza Hut in our neighborhood. You had your pick of local Italian joints. It could take an hour to get your pizza, but that was because it was a deep dish pizza and had to cook longer than the thin crust. It was usually something my mom would have gotten before she came to the house or a friend coming by later. I liked almost any kind of pizza that didn't have fish on it! I remember somebody came over and they bought a pizza for us one night, and it had anchovies on it. The pizza tasted salty and my sisters and brother and I couldn't figure it out. When they told us that it had anchovies on it, I decided that I wouldn't do that again to a pizza. I'll eat anchovies in a traditional Caesar salad dressing, or on some other Italian dishes, but never again on a pizza.

Another favorite was a Swedish smorgasbord styled restaurant. We always went there and we always got their Swedish meatballs, or at least I did. I had never had Swedish meatballs before and so that was one of the things I always ordered. It was also one of the first times I experienced a white table cloth restaurant. It was buffet-style and you know that was a treat for us. I also loved going to the pancake house too. I would get pancakes if we were there for breakfast, but if we were going in for a lunch or dinner I would get a club sandwich because I used to love to play with the toothpicks! The original toy with a meal! It really did not take much back in the day to amuse kids while dining. I wanted the toothpicks, and they had better be all four different colors. Don't give me all red or all yellow!

My father took us to this one restaurant in the city called Army & Lou's. It closed a few years ago, but it was the first upscale soul food restaurant I had ever been in. It was a Black owned business on the south side of Chicago. I considered it upscale because they had table-cloths and served good food on a plate at your table instead of in a box to go. I remember the first time I would ever see an onion ring that was between half and the quarter size of the onion. I thought I was an onion ring connoisseur at a young age too because we used to go to White Castle all the time and I would get my onion rings from there as well as making them at home. I know my onion rings now, but these rings were larger than onions you see in the store. And the catfish, instead of just throwing it in the basket and putting it out on a plate, they had a beautiful presentation and great service. We knew it was Black owned and that there were Black servers, so we just assumed that the cooks in the kitchen were Black too. But whoever was in there knew how to present food on a plate! Even at that age, I was appreciating the service of delivering good food presented well.

On Sundays there was this bakery we passed on the way to church called Bernie Brother's Bakery. You know, I've never been to it but it that was a wholesale bakery over on the west side of the city. We passed it every time we went to church because we lived in a western suburb and we had to drive all the way to the far south side to reach church. It probably should have been a 30-45 minute drive, but Mom had a heavy foot and she drove so fast that she got the drive down sometimes to about 25 minutes when she was hoofing it. Usually we were grateful for the quicker commute, but when she got close to that bakery I just wanted to ask her to slow down so that I could enjoy the smell of the bread baking. The smell just permeated that whole area and I don't think we were close to the facility. I don't remember seeing the signs for it but you just knew that it was around because the whole area smelled like bread baking. Every Sunday I would look forward to passing it.

I think the name of the church was Mozart Baptist Church on the city's west side. Mom sang in the choir. She used to drag us out on Sunday nights and Wednesdays nights to go to bible study class and her rehearsals. I really didn't like going to church on Sunday nights because it meant that we would miss Bonanza and whatever else was on television, and there was no such thing as a VCR or DVR to record shows for us at that time. But Sunday night service, or BTU, was not that bad. That was where I really learned more about the Bible because we had competitions that made us memorize the books of the bible and made me more familiar with the details of the Bible. It was more like Sunday school but at night because we were broken down into age groups.

I didn't really become active in church until we joined Christ Universal Temple. When I was in high school, I was a student teacher and my sister Judy was a teacher, she liked the babies. She always liked the babies so she went to the baby/preschool classroom and she'd hold the babies during the service. I didn't have time for that kind of drama. I wanted somebody with a little sense on them. I wanted third grade! At least they knew what I was talking about, and I had fun with them. While I was in grade school, I would go to church for first service, play around during and between services, and be an assistant Sunday school teacher during the second service. But when I was in high school, when I wasn't ogling the organist during Sunday Service, I would be a student teacher and be active in the high school group, Youth Expressing Christ (YEC).

We used to have our meetings during the second service. Judy, Paul and I were very active in that group. And mind you they were all people that we only met in church because we were not going to their schools, we were in the suburbs, and suburban and city kids didn't go to the same schools at all. Oh, my God, no… and even in that church group, there were kids from the west side, south side, and different high schools. At least at church everyone had to put down their rivalries because we didn't allow any of that drama at the church. We met a whole bunch of people definitely from different walks of life going to church.

The church was affiliated with different sister churches across the nation, and every summer there would be a conference for the YEC group, and that's how I ended up in New York for the first time. We took a chartered bus ride to New York to one of the sister church's locations and we spent a week in Pawlings, New York. I'll never forget it. A commuter train to the camp site where we would stay followed by a police escort. There were about one hundred or more of us Black high school kids walking through the neighborhood which was all white. That's not an experience you forget too soon.

Before we left Chicago, Reverend Doctor Johnnie Coleman, our African-American female minister, gave us a lecture about our behavior. "If you act up, they'll have the money to put you back here on the plane; I will be there to pick you up with your parents." Be a fool if you want to, but you knew exactly what she was talking about. She left us all thinking "Lord, I don't need to be meeting that when I get back home!" For the most part, I think everybody who was going to church in that group was pretty good. I don't remember any bad seeds being there. But this was the first time, and the last time, I had to get a police escort to walk through a neighborhood and all I could think was, "Oh, my God, really?" That was in the late seventies.

When we had our tour day through New York City, we broke up into groups of ten, we always had a group leader or a teacher with us. Even though I grew up in the Chicago area, I lived in the suburbs and hadn't really been in the city like this before. I remember seeing a White man and this Black woman walking towards each other and doing their own thing when their shoulders bumped each other in passing. The man turned around and starts cussing at the woman and the woman turns her head to yell not-so-flattering comments at the man, all without stopping. Both of them kept right on walking, they never stopped. That was my first introduction to New York City.

I became the President of the International Youth Expressing Christ, and I had my boyfriend going with me to the church and YEC at the time. I was voted in as the international president and at our local Chapter in my church I was the secretary. So, I was very active. I went from school teacher, to officer, to international officer. Most of my responsibilities as an international officer, including planning the next conference, took place at the conference. It was easier because we were all there together. We might make a couple of phone calls or something like that during the course of the year because we had people from Detroit, New York, from the Bahamas' area, I mean, we were kind of scattered. I did enjoy it though.

We didn't spend all our time eating out and at church. We spent a lot of time running around our neighborhood too. Across the street from us, there was an old white lady named Paula who was friends with my mom and would always take care of us. They used to swap the Sunday papers with each other. We used to get the Sun Times and she would get the Tribune, and they would swap them so that they didn't miss out anything important. She was the spinster lady that everybody in the neighborhood was scared of. It seemed like she would be mean to everyone else in the neighborhood except us. Whatever my sisters and brother and I wanted, we got. If the ball or Frisbee went into her yard by accident, we had to go get it because everyone else was too afraid of having her fuss at them. She had this fantastic garden with all these different kinds of flowers. I guess the other kids didn't respect her stuff as much as she wanted them to, so she wouldn't allow them to come into her yard. We could though. She was also the first person I ever saw drink coffee twenty-four-seven, she always had a coffee cup in her hand. It could be eighty degrees outside, and she'd have coffee up in her hand. She was a serious coffee drinker. She was also the first person I knew to drive a Volkswagen Bug. I'll never forget her for that.

As I'm sure you can tell, the neighborhood we lived in was mixed. But our immediate block, for the most part, was all Black. On the opposite corner, across the street, was the first time I would meet an interracially married couple. We're talking about the sixties or early seventies, a Black man married to a white woman and their two kids are living in our neighborhood. Of course we would hear people talking and sharing their unsolicited opinion on their relationship, but we didn't really have any problems with them. The kids were about Cheryl's age, or maybe years older than that, so it was not like we would hang out with them so much. Other than that one couple, our block was mainly Black, but you could go two blocks up, or the other side tracks of my suburban town and find the area with the higher mortgages, higher rents, and those areas tended to have more white families.

When we went from our town to the neighboring town of Melrose Park we always knew that while we were in there we had better behave. They were harder on Black people in that area than they were on white people. People always got pulled over or harassed when they went to the stores. There was this one shopping mall that we would all go to called Winston Park Plaza. Everyone went there because it was the only shopping strip on our side of town. There was a Woolworth's there that where I remember having a race related issue at the restaurant.

Mom and her three youngest were totally ignored while we were sitting at the table for lunch. We sat there for about fifteen minutes watching the waitresses going by and people coming in after us were getting served, before mom finally went to find a manager. Mom and the manager exchanged words and finally a waitress came over to take our order. "What do you want!" yelled the server in what I remember to be a rude tone. Even though Mom already told us that we were not going to eat there, Mom started to order and then told us to order what we wanted. "But you said we would leave," we protested. "Shut up! Order what you want. Just order what you want!" Mom hissed. And so we all ordered our food, and they put the order in. Because we were at a lunch counter styled restaurant, we could see them cooking, and as soon as she saw them cooking our order Mom said, "Ok, now we can leave."

By then we were really confused. "But we didn't get our food!" First she said we were not going to eat there, then she told us to order, and now she was saying we were going to leave. "We don't have our food." "Let's go!" Mom replied. That was the first time I ever walked out of a restaurant. Looking back, I realize that it was because we got crappy service and she was going to let them know that she didn't appreciate it. Fortunately, we didn't have too many race-related issues in our hometown, but that was one that stood out in my mind.

Back then, we knew how to act and where you could act up if you wanted to act up at all! Most of us learned it the hard way when a grown up conversation between a neighbor and your parents started with, "girl, I saw your child..." ended up with you getting whipped. You were not the only one raising your child. It's not so much like that now, but back in those days, anyone in the village would tell on you.

My mom didn't play. She didn't have to say, "wait 'til your daddy gets home." It was Momma handling business. And you didn't want to wait 'til Daddy came home anyway because he worked two jobs and when he came home he was already tired. Don't let Daddy come home and find out that you messed up! Oh no, no, no! I couldn't remember getting spanked, or we called it "whipped," by my daddy. She would tell you to get a switch, "let's go!" "I gotta go pick a switch?!" I used to think that if I got the little skinny one so that it would break off. But I soon learned that the little skinny thing hurt worse than the larger ones! There was even one time that I tried to hide the belt. "I have another belt!" Mom yelled when she couldn't find it.

I didn't get into too much trouble growing up, but I did earn my fair share of meetings with a switch or a belt. One of the things I used to get into trouble for was not being in the house when the street lights came on. When the streetlights came on, you were not supposed to be at the curb, in the driveway, or even at the front door, you were supposed to be *in* the house.

I remember another time when she whipped me because the clothes were still in the dryer. When Mommy got home she asked me if I had folded up all of the clothes, and I told her that I had. Unfortunately for me, during this conversation I forgot that when I pulled the laundry out of the dryer I left some of the clothes to run through another cycle because they were not dry yet. This forgotten minor detail ended up costing me because Mom thought I lied to her. She walked over to the dryer and found the clothes and tore me up.

I only tended to get into trouble for situations like those. It was not like we were talking back to her. None of us even thought about raising our tone or calling her out of her name. I honestly don't think the thought ever crossed my mind to do so. And it was not about grades because we all had good grades. I'm not saying that we always had perfect scores, but we always did well in school. We had a pretty good incentive program. Daddy paid for good grades.

Daddy paid $10 for an A, $5 for a B, but he didn't pay for C's. It's good money today for a school aged child, but that was *really* good money back in the day. It was tax free too! It helped me buy my favorite romance books and Barbie doll accessories. Mommy used to dress me and Judy alike, so every year we would get coats or dresses for Christmas. Judy's clothes would be blue and mine would be pink. We probably looked forward to getting our hands on the boxes as much as the coats and dresses, because they came in these big fold up boxes, about 3' x 5'. We would fold up those boxes and put our Barbie dolls and all the home furnishings, clothes and accessories under the bunk bed, and we would be good to go. That's what I spent a lot of my money on. I wish I knew where those Barbie doll houses and accessories were now because I could probably make some money off of them! But we didn't think about things like that back then.

In grade school it was easy to know where you stood in class long before your report card came out because each class was segregated by our academic performance. There were groups A, B, and C. It was the smart ones, the students in group A, who were put with the below average ones, the students in group C, as they needed some help. Every day we were reminded of our status as smart, average, or "other." Looking back, some people may think it was harsh, but at least it was a realistic representation of how we are treated in the real world, especially in the kitchen. We are segregated into different categories there too! I was in the smart group all of the time. Actually, all of my siblings were in smart group A. Everyone assumed the students in group B would be alright, so the focus was on helping the students in group C. By the time I was in fifth grade, I was going back to fourth grade helping the fourth graders who were in group C. It was nice to be able to get out of class every once and a while, but the real perk for being in group A was getting money from Daddy.

Back in the day we didn't have middle school. It was just grade school, kindergarten through eighth grade, and then high school. We walked to our grade school every day. I'm not saying that we walked up a hill both ways to school with a hole in our sock, but the schools were in the neighborhood and there were no buses, and so we were always walking to school—snow, rain, hail, sleet—it didn't matter. We walked to school, but it was only about five blocks away, straight down one street, so it was no big deal.

From kindergarten to sixth grade I went to a public school called Emerson Elementary. We were the Warriors and our colors were green and gold! Although I was pretty athletic in my school years, I didn't play any sports in elementary school because girls just didn't have sports teams yet in public schools. We did have Physical Education (PE) though. In Illinois, PE was required and at the beginning of the school year we bought uniforms to wear to PE every day. In addition to PE, we had an hour for lunch each day, so after we walked home for lunch, got our Chef Boy R Dee on, or at least some Campbell's soup or grilled cheese, we would walk back to school and still have 20 minutes left to play!

For seventh and eighth grade Mom put Paul and me into a private school because of an issue with one of his teachers. Back then, corporate punishment was still allowed in schools, and paddling was popular. Mom had an issue when a teacher decided to kick my brother. The teacher said that she had only used her foot to move him back into line, or something like that, but by the time news of the incident got to my mother she made her way up to the school faster than my father could get there. My momma decided that she wanted to kick the teacher back! Mom could raise all kind of hell when she was ready. There was also another teacher there that she didn't like who taught 5th grade. Mom didn't like her habit of calling kids stupid or dumb and how mean the teacher would be towards people sometimes. So the next year we were in a private school.

The private school we went to was called Saint Paul Lutheran. It was in neighboring suburb of Melrose Park. The majority of the students in that school were white, so things were a little racially charged. Our walk to the private school was about a mile long because Mom didn't pay for me and my brother to ride the bus. Sometimes we were lucky enough to be in a carpool.

I was not happy about the switch because in public school we were able to switch classrooms between classes, like the grown folks in high school. I also remember being frustrated because I missed out on the coveted eighth grade trip to DC held every Spring break. I ended up going camping with the kindergarteners instead of going to DC with my childhood friends.

I can't say that private school was *all* bad because I had my first "boyfriend" in eighth grade. We were not necessarily dating in the sense that we would spend time at the movies or have dinner out together after school but we did call ourselves boyfriend and girlfriend for a time. Momma didn't allow any us to date. She would have shut that down! Even though I knew I was risking getting in trouble with Mom, I fell for the phrase that paid back in the day, "give me a chance." So we were an item for a little while, but it didn't last too long because after two years of mile-long school commutes Mom put us into a public high school where I became a Proviso East Pirate sporting the blue and white.

By the time I got to high school, Title IX came out and I was able to play more sports. All of us were athletic. No, I take that back. My oldest sister was not athletic, but the rest of us were. I played softball, I played basketball, and I ran track. My brother ran cross-country. Judy played badminton and softball. All three of us girls were color guards, but that was back before you had all that twirling and stuff they do now. We didn't have all those big and fancy flags, we just had a couple little flags. It was not as high-tech as it is now, but we had our nice military styled uniforms. We were a good, high-stepping looking good squad too!

The irony is that I got into sports so that I could get out of the kitchen. During the holidays, my family always hosted celebrations and we all spent hours in the kitchen preparing food, cleaning the house, and getting dressed. The preparation was long and tedious but the final results were always well received. Whenever one of the Brock's threw a party, it was always well attended because everyone knew that they would eat well, drink well, and be entertained. So when I had enough of chopping and cleaning in the kitchen, I would tell my mom that I was going to go "entertain the company," which, for me, consisted of sitting myself in front of the TV and watch one of the games with the guys because the women were all in the kitchen. To maintain my cover I would occasionally offer the men and their sons a drink or a relish tray full of deviled eggs, pickles and olives and play the role of the little hostess, all to avoid being in the kitchen chopping, cooking, cleaning. One of the unanticipated side effects of this habit was that I began to understand and enjoy football at a very young age. It amazes me still today that a lot of guys don't realize that there are women who really like football and know exactly what's going on, sometimes better than they do! I have caught a lot of people off guard like that. I never tried to play football though. My mother was a Chicago Bulls fan, and my father was a sports person too. I could sit there for hours with my dad and watch the Cubs play on channel 9. That was back in the day when the Cubbies played only in the daytime. Although I used sports to get me out of the kitchen, I still loved the kitchen even then.

Cooking is a rush. It's a pleasure, truly to know that you can cook and prepare something for someone that they will really like. Whether they could or couldn't cook for themselves, being able to put something together, be it as simple as a burger or something more complex like a beef wellington, and make a nice meal for them that they will truly appreciate and will talk about days or weeks later is a good feeling. I don't consider myself to be artistic at all! I mean, I draw some crooked straight people. But cooking is an art form, so if I'm artistic then food is my medium. I can tell you how it should be on the plate. I can do that all day. But don't ask me to draw. It's not my forte.

Culinary inspirations came in abundance: my mom's good cooking, the restaurants we went out to eat at, and two cooking shows on PBS—The Galloping Gourmet and Julia Childs. The star of the show *The Galloping Gourmet* was Graham Kerr. I didn't know what his name was until I was well in my 40's. I would be enthralled with watching this guy, with this funny accent who I couldn't place where he came from at that point in time. I guessed that he was of British or Australian desent because of his classic English accent. All I knew for sure was that he was not originally from Chicago. And then to see a man in the kitchen cooking like that was unfamiliar to me too. I couldn't even tell you what things that he cooked on the show. I just remember watching him, and being fascinated from seeing him whizzing through the kitchen because he was always, well, like the title of the show, galloping through the kitchen! He was always moving and doing something in the kitchen that I had never seen before. I guess you could say that it was his personality that fascinated me almost more than the cooking. At least it was at first.

Then there was Julia Childs with this other accent, hers sounded French. She'd have the little beverage in her hand sometimes while she cooked or right when she would sit down at the table to eat. No one can describe what it was like watching her better than the famous skit from Saturday Night Live with Dan Aykroyd when he did his now infamous Julia Childs. He wore an apron and spoke in a high-pitched voice when he suddenly exclaims that he, or his character Julia Childs that is, has cut her hand and has blood gushing everywhere. Once Julia realizes that she has cut herself, she responds by pouring a little sherry into the dish she's preparing and drinking some herself. "Oh, I've cut my hand! Oh, put a little sherry there, a little sherry for me." I remember watching that with my brother because we would watch Saturday Night Live at a young age, and you know just watching those skits and he's impersonating her and oblivious she is to how she hurt herself! It was so funny because I remember her cutting something a couple of times on the show and saying "Oh! I cut my…Oh, not quite." It was different just to see that kind of food because it was not necessarily food that we were eating at home. We didn't eat Beef Bourguignon. My Easy-Bake Oven was not doing anything like that!

It might have been watching those shows that inspired me to try new recipes when it was my turn to cook. When I was trying a new recipe cooking didn't seem like a chore, it was something I looked forward to. When I was growing up, you were expected to clean your plate no matter what was fixed for dinner, so it was nice to at least give my family something new to eat. There was no playing at the table, if I put this on your plate, you will eat it. I'll admit there were nights when I was left sitting right there at the table two hours later still staring at some food on my plate that I didn't like. It was funny because there were two things that my mother would fix that I was just not going to eat. I even tried to trick myself into eating it by hiding it in mashed potatoes and eating it, but it didn't work. I would sit there and try to be slick by giving it to the dog, but even the dog wouldn't eat it. I hate canned asparagus to this day. I love asparagus, fresh. But don't feed me canned asparagus. That's some nasty stuff. And, I still don't like okra.

She would throw it in some greens, throw it in the cabbage, throw it in some succotash, or anything else she could think of. On those nights I would pick out all of the food around the asparagus or okra and leave it right there on the plate. Everyone would have cleared all the dishes and put all the food away while I was still sitting there looking at whoever was cleaning up. After all of that, sometimes I would get my butt whipped, sometimes I was just might get sent to bed, and sometimes I would just get fussed at. It was a variable. Of course I never liked the punishment, but I just couldn't eat it. I just knew I would ralph.

I'll admit that there was one time that I ate okra, since I've become an adult, and loved it. A Chef made it for me by mixing tamarind and other Indian spices that changed the flavor of it. The okra was cut into lengthwise slivers and quickly fried or sautéed so that it was crispy. After he did all of this, at least it was edible.

With the exception of my love-to-hate relationship with canned asparagus and okra, my early experiences with food began to point towards a career once I reached high school. My high school was a closer walk than the private school I had attended for seventh and eighth grades. We lived on 9th Avenue, the public grade school I had attended was on 4th Avenue, and the high school I went to was on 1st Avenue. Thanks to Title IX, the school had to build a sport complex for the girls, to match the boy's field house, locker rooms, weight rooms, and everything else. Our complex was called Memorial Hall. It had a pool and a gymnasium and the music & band classes were held there. We had golf and just about every other sport you could think of at the school. But with all of the sport activities I enjoyed during high school, I didn't have any of them represented on my high school class ring. On my class ring I had a symbol for home economics.

The stats are that the majority of cooking classes were filled with minorities. Men and women of color are getting trained, but are not getting the culinary positions. Once I learned about the culinary world, my aspirations were never to be a cook, I studied to learn to be a Chef, and I learned about the culinary world through my home economics classes in high school. I took every cooking class they had. The microwave was new back then, and that was the first place I saw a microwaved turkey. It was ugly looking because it didn't have any brown on it. It was done, but it was still a blonde looking turkey!

I took a total of four classes. I don't even know what they call it anymore, but I remember that I took my beginner classes with Ms. Adams and my two advanced classes with Ms. Dennis. I remember taking Ms. Dennis' class because there was one white girl in the class whose name was Kim too. On the morning that Ms. Dennis returned our last test for the semester she announced that there was one "A" in the class and challenged us to guess who it belonged to. Everyone guessed Kim. Then Ms. Dennis said, "Well, it was Kim but it was not that Kim, it was Kim Brock." What?! I had earned 98 points out of 100 possible points. Everyone was shocked, because I was quiet and I kept to myself, but I aced her test. She was surprised, and I was surprised too. I was also excited because it was a school policy that if you aced the test you would be exempt from the final. That was one less test I had to study for!

There was another home economics course I took, but it was more of a course of interior decorating and fashion. I don't remember the teacher's name, but I remember that she was surprised that I knew what a pillow sham and duster were. She was a white lady and most of her students were Black, and for most of my classmates she was the first to introduce them to pillow shams, dusters, and other interior decorator architectural terms. Even though we drank Tang all the time and I never had a full piece of bacon until I was grown and living on my own, my mom knew how to stretch a buck so that we could have food and pillow shams! I also remember the class because I had her class when I was 16, and that's when my father died. The week he died I took a week off from school and all my other activities. She started worrying about me because I didn't usually miss school, but someone in the class told her why I was absent. She was very supportive during that trying time.

It was in my junior year of high school when my dad died. I was sixteen at the time, so this was about ten years after he and my mom divorced and he became more of a "weekend dad." During my freshman year he moved out west to the California area and remarried, so during that time we didn't see him. We never even met his new wife. But that marriage only lasted about a year and then he came back during my sophomore year.

I did more than play sports and cook during high school. I was also a party planner. Well, sort of. I joined the student council my senior year. I don't remember if it was my sister or someone else who was older than me, but someone told me to join the council so that I could have a say about the prom and make sure we didn't have a sorry prom. This was during the seventies, so there was some racial tension because two different cultures wanted to have a prom that represented them. The white kids wanted to have their bands and their music and the Black kids wanted their own bands too.

Our proms were totally different back then. We ended up having our prom at the Hyatt Regency Hotel at O'Hare airport. It was a sit down dinner with three or four courses. I don't remember what we had for dinner that night, but I remember that our theme was "Stairway to Heaven." It was already an old song by that time, but that was the theme we all chose. We went through all these songs, but even though rap was just starting to become popular, we didn't want Sugarhill Gang at our sit down dinner. It was a mixed school, so when everyone gave their opinion "Stairway to Heaven" because, "Ain't no stopping us now" was one of those popular prom songs and we had to be different.

If you spoke to the eight or nine year old version of me and asked, "What do you want to be when you grow up?" I don't think I would've said cook because I didn't know about that when I was that age. I would've said I wanted to go to college. What did I want to do in college? I had no clue at that point. I know I never said doctor, lawyer, or anything like that. I just always knew I was going to grow up, and I would go away to school because that's what they did in the books—go away to college.

Mom and Dad always said, "You're going to go to college," so combining that with all the Nancy Drew and Hardy Boys stories about roommates who would always sneak in and do different things, I just knew that I wanted to be college bound and experience dorm life. It turns out that I'm the only one out of the four who didn't go to college and have a dorm life though because I ended up at a junior college. But after hearing enough of my sibling's roommate horror stories, I've decided that I have not missed out on anything worth regretting.

I was fresh out of high school with no bills and not too many cares in the world. I left my high school sweetheart and all that was home or a representation of life in "Big D" with my oldest sister. I was ready for a change in my life. I was ready to do something different. I was ready to meet new people and get going on what I would do for my career. There was never any doubt in my mind that I would have a career, I just didn't know what it would be. At the time, I thought I was too stressed to go straight to college. It was not until much later that I would find out what "too stressed" would feel like!

Although I was already accepted to a few colleges, I didn't have the finances to attend any of them. At the time, I had no clue how to apply for financial aid or what the steps were to get financial aid. My mother was not able to help on the subject and my father had already died. My sisters were not there to tell me and my high school counselor was none existent. I was really interested in a university in

Tennessee because my sister Judy, who had already been my roommate for most of my life, was already in the state going to college. It would be great to be close to her again yet far enough to have my own experiences, or at least this was my thinking at the time. But life has a way of changing your course and direction sometimes. It just was not meant to be that way.

I knew I needed money to pay my fair share of expenses and to have fun while exploring life in the city. The Social Security check I was getting was going to be stopped if I didn't enroll in school full time. I looked at schools in the Dallas/Fort Worth area and didn't find anything that moved me enough to consider them. So I found a job in the paper and applied at a Holiday Inn as a waitress for the morning shift. Talk about a new experience!

I had never waited tables before in my life. Thanks to the times my family and I went out to eat, I was at least familiar with what good service looked like. I will never forget the time my mom had us walk out of a restaurant because of the lack of service, or when my dad took my sister and I to a diner in downtown Chicago after watching the movie "The Sting". The waitress followed her two customers out of the restaurant and threw their tip, a few coins back at them as they were walking away and yelled that they must have needed the money more than she did. I may not have had experience as a waitress, but at least I had a couple of examples of what not to do. There would be many other times in my life when I would rely on my personal experiences to show me what not to do!

I ended up in Dallas when I went to visit my sister Cheryl for a summer and never left. So here I was an 18 year old waiting tables and earning more money than my college educated sister. A slow shift would net $70 a day! Some of the men would slip me an extra bill when their dining companion was not looking or there would mysteriously be a ten dollar bill on the floor underneath the table on his side. After a while, I picked up some dinner shifts and started helping out at the bar. Although I was legal to drink (yes, 18 year olds were allowed to drink at that time) I was not familiar with the bar scene, so I had no idea what was going on when people would place an order for 7&7 or Bourbon and Branch. Fortunately, the other staff members covered me on that one.

The staff was pleasant and it was pretty much a "family" environment. The Food & Beverage director had his family working there in various capacities-hosting, bussing tables, tending to the bar, and whatever else that got them paid. On a few occasions the head Chef would be late to work and we would scramble trying to get breakfast out. Luckily one of the waitresses knew how to cook a little and was at least able to get the morning started.

While working there I became interested in how those big stoves and ovens worked. I had never been around a flat top or grill before. I had never flipped an egg in a skillet or used a salamander to broil. The first time I did flip an egg for an order, it was supposed to be over easy with the yolks intact. Half of my flipped egg landed in the pan and the rest was on the burner. I killed several orders before I was able to get that trick down! My interest was piqued and the Executive Chef was more than willing to train me on how to help with opening the kitchen in the mornings. Between this and my experience with food growing up and the cooking class in high school, my curiosity was growing.

While reading the paper one day, I came across a featured article about a student from the local community junior college who had graduated from a culinary apprenticeship program. The photo was showing them in the kitchen and talking about how the three year culinary apprenticeship program was helping to make a Chef out of them. That struck me as something I definitely wanted to do! I called the number listed and got an interview lined up at the school with the culinary director and local executive Chefs who were running the apprenticeship program.

I don't recall them turning anybody down or rejecting anybody. It was like an alchemy test. We had to taste and smell different things to see if we could identify them, there was also a written test. They wanted to know if the food we were sampling was salty, sweet, or bitter. We were asked, "How does this smell? Do you know what this is?" They do that also a couple of times on the television show

"Hell's Kitchen," where they are blindfolded and they have to taste something, the test I took did the same thing.

I learned then that we really do eat with our eyes, because if you try eating something, even if it's something common, while you are blindfolded it will throw you off. A lot of people look at something and say, "I don't like it." You have not even tried it, but "I don't like it." It has to do with how well your palette and senses are developed. For example, if I gave you a kumquat, would you know that it is a kumquat, or would you think it's just an orange, or a lemon? Or if I gave you an Asian Pear, would you notice the difference or would you think it would just be a pear? It's like an apple, but with a totally different texture, taste, and look. Of course, I didn't know any of this at the time I took the test.

I got the bitter and sour part right. Lord have mercy! Bitter and sour are two memorable tastes! I think it was the salty one that gave me trouble. I don't like salty. I am not a salty person. It was something I had an issue with. Bitter versus sour is difficult because what might be sour for you might be bitter for me, or vice versa. Is a lemon sour or bitter to you? Most people assume sour, but if you eat the pith then that makes it bitter.

It was a matter of the test and meeting some of the teachers- the Chefs from the American Culinary Federation (ACF), and getting acclimated to the school and what the program was all about. You know, they explained it all to us. The professional kitchens they put us in were on a completely different level from the kitchens we cooked in at home and in home economics classes in high school! The difference between cooking in my home economics class and being in the culinary arts program was like night and day. The new school had bigger and better professional grade, quality equipment. There were things in their kitchen that I had never seen or worked with before! They had broilers, salamanders, grills and flat tops, convection ovens instead of conventional ovens or combo ovens. Even the equipment I did recognize was on a different level. For example, we didn't just have mixers, we had floor model mixers with 60 quart or 120 quart bowls.

Everything about the structure of the program was different from high school, but I was ready. The shortest distance between two points may be a straight line, but my journey from cooking my father's breakfast to enrolling in an ACF culinary program was not a straight path. But the path I took allowed me to pick up all the things I would need to be successful.

CHAPTER 2

Mis en Place

There's nothing like being in a new environment to find out what you are really made of. In Maywood I knew the layout of the neighborhood, I knew the people to trust and who not to trust. But going to a culinary arts program in Dallas was a whole different ball game. I had Cheryl there to help me navigate the geography and the social scene of the city, but even my four high school cooking classes didn't prepare me for the new language, structure, and culture of the culinary arts program. Once I jumped into the culinary world I realized that it would take every lesson that my upbringing equipped me with to be able to navigate this new domain. Now was the time to find out what I was really made of.

I signed up for three long years of minimum wages when I enrolled at the local community college to work in an industry I knew nothing about. As an ACF apprentice I was earning $6 an hour. It may not look like a big difference to you, but that was a difference I could feel! The ACF apprenticeship program was luckily alive and doing well in graduating experienced cooks, so I was hopeful.

We were told in the beginning of our program that Chefs liked to steal apprentices from the program before the three years are up whenever they found a young hopeful that could help them advance their own careers as Chefs instead of encouraging the apprentice to complete the program to begin a more promising career of their own. As I progressed in the program I saw how easy it would be to quit and go for the extra .50 cents or more an hour in pay. For those students who needed the money to live, it was a hard choice. For me, it was a no brainer. I am not one to quit and I had little expenses to cover.

All of us were required to participate in a three year apprenticeship so that we could have experience in all of the different parts of the kitchen, so the earlier we got started on it the sooner we could graduate. With this in mind, I started working in the kitchen before our classes started because classes didn't start until September and I started the program during the summer. Many of the program's graduates worked in hotels because, at the time, that was the only place that had all of the different parts we were to be trained on. The butcher shop, the different types of restaurants for breakfast, lunch, and dinner, bake shop, pastry shop, and everything in between. We were going to be trained to do it all!

My first choice of where I was going to work was a hotel at the airport. I was fascinated by the whole prospect of working with the airlines as well as for the hotel. It also gave me flying benefits and as soon as I learned about this I started making plans on how I would use them! Then the reality of not having my own transportation to get me to and from work started to settle in. I had no car and there was no public transportation, at the time, to the airport. So I settled for the second option received.

My apprenticeship was at the Hyatt Regency Dallas, and the first kitchen position I worked in was Garde-manger, the cold kitchen. Working at the Hyatt gave me many life lessons. It was my first time seeing a Black person in charge of a department, my first time dealing with sexism and sexual harassment, my first time dealing with a temperamental Chef or being around workers who had no hope or dreams of being or having more. The Hyatt taught me the difference between having a career versus having a job.

While there I repeatedly saw female cooks and Sous Chefs passed over for promotion because "he" was better. Now there were definitely some situations when this could be objectively proven, but after you

26

see it happen time and time again it will give you a reason to pause and reflect on your career choice. Rarely seeing someone who looks like you, be it be race or gender, in a position of authority or in management can be disheartening as well.

While at the Hyatt, I also learned how I wanted to manage by witnessing other managers in action. I swore I wouldn't be like this one or that one. One of those Chefs I vowed not to imitate was the first Chef I met when I began my apprenticeship in the Garde-manger. We all referred to the Chef over the Garde-manger as "The Snake." It was sad, really, because he was the first Black man I had seen in a Chef's uniform and he was truly a snake. He was a preacher on Sunday and would raise hell Monday through Saturday. This man was about 6'2" and his body was always in the shape of a boomerang because he always walked hunched over. He's the kind of manager that would get in your face to make it personal when he yelled at you in his loud booming voice, "Why is this cut up? And why is this displayed on this tray? Did I tell you to put blue? I told you to put red! And why is it looking like that instead of turning it this way? And why didn't you do this? And didn't I tell you..." The worst part is that he would stay in your face and keep yelling at you until you started to tear up and then he would fall back and walk off as if he did nothing wrong.

If learning to manage public humiliation was part of the training, then he was definitely the best teacher in that area. The Garde-manger area was right next to the banquet kitchen and saucier, the place where the sauces are made, and there was no wall to separate the areas. So when it was your turn to be berated and belittled by The Snake, you had about 50 other people hearing about your mistake. He would yell at you for almost anything, maybe the lettuce was not cut fine enough, your jello was not right, your cheese was not cut right, or maybe you didn't complete everything within the time frame he thought it should have been done, it didn't matter. But when he was done the student was usually beet red and crying while they tried to continue working to fix the mistake. I only remember him doing that to me one time, because no one could get out of it if you worked for him. And no one ever came over to try to help you in

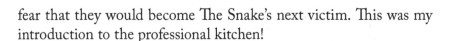

fear that they would become The Snake's next victim. This was my introduction to the professional kitchen!

The "snake" part of his name was less about his enjoyment with publicly humiliating students as it was about him trying to make up for the humiliation by trying to date his students. I guess after raising all that hell in the kitchen he needed a way to relax and his wife and kids didn't quite do it for him. After work he would find his way to the side of one of the female apprentices and offer to give you a ride. By the time he tried that line on me I had already heard about his scheme from the other women so the only words I had for him was, "No thank you, I'll walk."

Besides the humiliation factor of working with the man who yelled in your face all the time, the Garde-manger area stands out in my memory because of the people who worked there with me. The area was full of women. There were no men who worked in that particular kitchen. Thanks to Texas being near the border, we had Mexican and Black women in the kitchen. That department was unique because it was the only one I have seen that was run the whole time by Black leaders. Although the Snake was there during the day, there was a manager who was a Black female, and another younger Black woman who worked during the nighttime, for a total of two people on the night shift. They would finish up any dishes or parties we didn't complete during the day to make sure all the platters we needed for hotel parties would be ready on time. During my apprenticeship I learned how to work a 60 hour week and still go to classes in the evening. I honestly preferred going to classes in the evening anyway because the morning classes were just too early. There were times when I my only option was to take classes in the morning, but at least the Hyatt and the school worked together to make sure I had time to do both because of course I wouldn't have been at the Hyatt at all if I was not a student, so we had to make the classes work. I have not seen another team that was all female, Black managed and Black and Hispanic operated.

The Garde-manger did all the prep work and set up the fruit, cheese, salad, or canapé platters for parties. We prepped for three restaurants within the hotel. We would be the ones to set up the lettuces and whatever else they needed for the pantry in the restaurant. It may sound easy, but for banquets we may plate salads for about 800 people on the night of the event. It became even more interesting when a waiter rushed into the kitchen to grab the cheddar cheese platter but takes the goat cheese platter by mistake. It's even worse if the waiter sees a line of plated meals and confuses the $15 platter and a $200 platter. If this happens, you will have one customer who is really excited about the upgrade and a furious customer on the other side of the ballroom!

I enjoyed doing decorations and centerpieces with Garde-manger, especially in food shows and competitions. Hot plates shown cold, cold plates, and ice carvings were classic Garde-manger dishes, but I didn't learn how to do ice carving with The Snake because there was a Banquet Sous Chef who did the ice carvings. Even without the ice carving skills I mastered enough of the Garde-manger skills to place second in my first cooking competition.

We were required to participate in three competitions a year in Dallas, and my first one was a Sysco food show. I called it a "dead dough" competition. I was challenged to make bread dough without yeast. To shape it and mold it to make it look like molded object made out of baked bread. It would be good for things like holding rolls and other baked goods. I did mine using a skillet and I was so proud of it because I had never done that before. One of the Sous Chef's at the Hyatt took pity on me and taught me how to do it. Imagine having to publicly display your 3 month old learned skill and be judged for it. Intimidating to say the least or very rewarding at best.

For the hot food shown cold portion I used aspic, a classic Garde-manger ingredient. You could take a flank steak, prime rib, or tenderloin and slice it into five pieces, aspiced them all, and then fanned them out onto a plate. Aspic is really clear, unflavored gelatin that keeps the air out to preserve the fresh look of the food and makes it look shiny. Because it's gelatin, it is edible, but it is usually just used for display and you're not encouraged to eat it. After you aspic and arrange the meat you add whatever accoutrements or garnishments you want to help accentuate the meat. So if it's a tenderloin beef, a scored mushroom or potato might be used to show off the meat. The plate must be clean and everything on the plate must be symmetrical. If you have five slices, then you better have five garnishes and five this and five that. The meat has to be the right colored temperature too. It has to be right, or at least *look* right. I usually did savory competitions and threw in things I learned from Garde-manger, and I always placed during those competitions. I always thought that just by participating in the competition you were a winner anyway because there are so many cooks and Chefs who won't compete that those who are willing to compete are already winners just for participating!

After Garde-manger, the next area of the kitchen my apprenticeship introduced me to was the Saucier. I worked with a German Chef named Kurt. He was a nice enough man, but please don't make him mad! Oh my God. He could make some soups that I had never heard of, and I thought I was pretty good as far as my knowledge and culinary prowess goes. We would make soups about 50 gallons at a time, and he could have everything seasoned perfectly, even at those proportions. At that time we would make our own stocks, so there would usually be two kettles filled with bones and vegetable parts and the other ones would be used to make some kind of soup or chili.

Kurt's accent definitely made things interesting. "Ya, ya, go to the storeroom and get me some azzperahgus." "You want some what?" I would reply. "Azzperahgus," he would shout again in his thick German accent. He would send me to the storeroom and I didn't have a clue what he wanted. The other cooks and apprentices would just be falling out laughing. I didn't like asking him to repeat himself more than three times because then I would get a cursing out in German that I didn't want. Besides, it was too funny to hear him go off in his German accent and I was afraid I would start smiling or laughing and make him even more upset!

Kurt taught me how to make basic soups and the mother sauces. Back then we made everything from scratch, so I really learned a lot that helped me later at the banquet station. I also got a firsthand view of quantity cooking and plating. In a single day we may have to prepare for a banquet of 500, then a banquet for 200 followed by one for 30. You learn quickly how to keep things organized.

The next station I worked in was the Banquet kitchen. In the Banquet kitchen, you're talking about mass production and plating food for all the hotel banquets. Whether it was for a sorority function, a wedding, a group of doctors, or whoever, they wanted their food done right and they wanted it on time and the hot food better be hot and the cold food better be cold. And if you're really good, you will put a garnish on the plates too. There is a trick to getting that chicken, the sauce, the vegetable, and the starch on the plate and looking good and keeping it hot so that it's still hot at 12, even though you put it on the plates at 11. You have to undercook the chicken to a point, but to know how much to undercook the chicken you have to calculate how long the plates will sit in the hot boxes waiting to be served so that you will know how much the hot box will cook the chicken. When you are calculating, don't forget that chicken is done at 165 degrees and that the plates themselves come out of a warmer and their temperature will affect how fast the chicken will cook in the hot box. In that regard, experience is a great teacher.

Banquet kitchen definitely required some skill, but the skills I learned there didn't help me much in my baking and pastry class. My baking and pastry class was my worst class because I had no experience in it whatsoever. I had no clue about anything going on in that classroom. It's not like I was eating European tortes or things like that when I went out or while I was growing up. My instructor for the class was a French pastry Chef from one of the local hotels. He spoke very little English, so he brought his assistant pastry Chef with him to translate. I think the assistant wanted to be French, because he always spoke his English with a French accent.

When I started that class, I had no clue what he was talking about, but he tried to teach us about brulee, petit fours, and every other food and dessert that every young French child grows up on and most young American children can't pronounce. My response to the introduction of a new food was, "I'm sorry, what is a bru who?" I didn't really ask the question because I didn't want to embarrass myself. I should have asked and I probably would have received answers that would help me catch on sooner. Eventually it got to the point where the Chef couldn't make it to class because he got so busy with his job. Back in that day, it was understood that we had a 10 minute rule. If the teacher was not in the class 10 minutes after the class was scheduled to start, we would all sign the roll and leave. It happened one time too many and the Chef was fired. After that, someone from the school took over, but he was not a pastry Chef and we lost the opportunity to learn about baking and pastry. He knew some of the basics, but it was not the same.

We should have learned to make cakes, genoise, tortes, chocolate truffles, and different icings, fillings, and pastry creams. Instead, I learned this on the job through my apprenticeship. I made the pastry shop my last station in my apprenticeship because the Pastry Chef, a German man named was pure evil. I've heard people say that vertically challenged men walk around with a chip on their shoulder, I don't know if that's true all the time but it was definitely true for him! He was temperamental and then some. He was also known for having tantrums and throwing pots, pans, or worse. If an event changed at the last minute, or really if anything happened that he didn't like, he would spew so much hate and anger at his co-workers and the hotel staff that he wouldn't stop until he had to upchuck in the kitchen sinks.

Back in the day you could get away with a lot more things, if those things happened today he would go to jail. He would throw things on the floor or across the room at you. He would throw food, chairs, utensils, or whatever he could get his hands on. He didn't throw anything at me, but I did hear stories and see him during some of his tirades. I made the pastry shop my last stop in my three year apprenticeship because I was already intimidated by the class I took and because that man was a fool.

Fortunately, by the time it was my turn in the rotation to go to the pastry shop he took a job somewhere else and one of his assistants, an American guy named David took over. He was a very creative, cool, and laid back guy. He also had the mentality to teach you how to do what you needed to do. However, he was the one to make a comment that, looking back, should have made me think twice about my career choice. "Well, if I show you how to do this, I'm not gonna waste my time cause you're gonna get married and have babies and not do this anymore, am I?" "No, I'm not having any babies. " My reaction was not one of indignation and shock, because at the time I was determined not to have children. "I want to learn this. Come on and teach me." I was about 22 or 23 at the time, and my plan was to work, graduate, then get married when I was 25, and have twins when I was 27. When I actually turned 25 years old I decided that I was nowhere near ready to get married, but at age 22 and 23 that was my plan.

I met a lot of chauvinistic characters in the kitchen, but even with this memorable comment I wouldn't consider my Pastry Chef one of them. I understood where he was going with the comment. At that time, most women would go to college to meet their future husband so they can settle down and get married. That was never my train of thought. I wouldn't have tried to pay my own way through college just to find a husband! I wanted a career. I wouldn't want to take the time to train someone if I thought they were just going to do this for another year and then become a cook at Waffle House or something. I understood his point. But it was still a conversation that should not have happened that way. But look at it this way, this was a conversation I had with someone I don't really consider to be chauvinistic in his attitude towards women, so can you image the kinds of conversations I had with the men who were outright chauvinistic in the kitchen?

Of course there were those guys who believed a woman's place was in the pantry, Garde-manger or pastry kitchen. Women couldn't handle the grill or saute' at the middle station where all of the action was. The heat of the battle each night was not for women neither was the higher pay that went with it. Women were not made for the heat because they couldn't make the cut. At some point I started to believe them. Why else would the broiler be so high up on the walls? Or the grill made to be so wide that you couldn't reach to the back of it without getting your arm seared from the flames dancing below? Women were only good enough for the so-called "girly" jobs as in chopping lettuce or fruits and making salads in Garde-manger or icing cakes and plating desserts in pastry. That kind of work, at least, was considered more feminine and genteel by some and was of

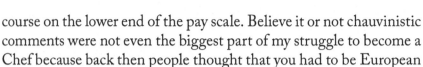

course on the lower end of the pay scale. Believe it or not chauvinistic comments were not even the biggest part of my struggle to become a Chef because back then people thought that you had to be European to be a great Chef, and then a male.

Europeans were always perceived to be better cooks. I really began to understand this when I went to the Culinary Olympics in 1984 as part of class field trip. It was a big upset when the Americans won a medal over a French, Swiss, or Austrian team. Those countries where known for their fine food and are the creators of the classics we eat today. All of the finest foods were believed to come from their countries, so no one believed that the American's should be able to win against them. But what the American teams realized was that when they start cooking their own regional foods they had a better chance of showing off their skill sets and winning. It was great to see our team win some of the events, but there is still a gradual shift towards valuing American cuisine. Life in the kitchen as an African-American who is a female was definitely interesting.

Now, when I went into the bake and pastry shop for my apprenticeship rotation I didn't go in thinking that I would become a Pastry Chef. Once you get past all the chauvinistic guys on the line who thought that women were only good for Garde-manger or pastry, I liked working in savory for the restaurants because I could hold my own on the line. Besides, after being dazed and confused in my pastry class, and then losing the instructor before the end of the course, how could I make plans to be a Pastry Chef?! But I stuck with it anyway because the Pastry Chef I worked with during my apprenticeship was a great teacher and I was doing well with it.

I never made the rotation into the butcher shop. My Chef didn't think it was necessary even though it was required and I would be tested on how to skin and filet a whole fish and on how to break down a cut of beef for serving. Truthfully, the shop had that old dried blood smell and was very cold. I'll even admit that the bain saw scared me. The site of the butchers sawing the sides of beef and breaking down the carcasses was fascinating to watch, but I was not inspired to do it! I had heard the horror stories of people losing fingers and digits to the saw. My father lost a part of his finger on one of his jobs too. I was not exactly interested in making this a family tradition.

I would just have to get through the practical test on whatever I learned in class or saw them doing in the butcher shop. The examiner for my final exam noticed how inept I was at butchering and outright asked me if I had ever spent time in the butcher shop. I had to tell him the truth. My Chef didn't think it was women's work and that my time would be better spend in the bake shop or wherever there was a shortage. Like I said, I didn't mind because I had no ambition to become the hotel's head butcher anyway.

On my exit interview with HR I was asked why I logged so many overtime hours in the bake shop, they didn't expect to see so many 60 hour weeks. I explained to the director, who was in administration for the culinary arts program as well and was not a Chef, the same thing that I have had to explain to many others along my journey. That in baking and pastry we start with raw ingredients. We then make a product from those raw ingredients. Whether it was a cake, pie, bread, or a type of cream, a lot of work went into producing them. The decorations, sauces, fillings, icings, and whatever else is needed to properly execute the dish to the highest standards. After all of that is done, we then have to garnish, cut, and plate the item as needed. Whereas in the savory side of the kitchen, the meat comes already portioned and cleaned so that all they have to do is season and cook it. So in the savory side of the kitchen there are 2 or 3 steps involved in preparing a dish, but in the pastry shop we have 5 to 7 steps. And that takes a lot more hours. This was a large part of the reason I was not ready to get married at age 25 either.

Even then I realized that it would be difficult to succeed in this profession with kids. Putting in 6-day, 60 hour weeks does nothing to help you raise a family. Men have a certain responsibility in raising a family too, but it really affects a woman more, of course, because of the general expectations of what a mother is supposed to do or be for her family.

Life as an apprentice was good. I made friends with people from all backgrounds. I didn't know any openly gay people or illegal residents growing up, but I did make friends with both openly gay and illegal residents while there in Dallas. I was relieved when I first realized that being around them was like being around anybody else. We all had issues and having a love life was complicated enough without public scorn added to it. Although I had resisted it in high school under the pretense that English was hard enough to master, I finally learned to speak some Spanish too. I secretly wish that I had taken a course or two back in high school because I may have had the foundation to learn more words from my friends than the few words I know now.

Combining book knowledge with job experience is a winning combination. Keeping your wits and composure when all around you are losing theirs is the key to a successful career in this or any business. One of our restaurant managers learned the significance of keeping your composure and not flying off the handle after she spent the morning berating the cooks and was later rewarded with a sandwich that was seasoned with a little technique called sweeping-the-floor-with-your-sandwich. Being open and receptive to other point of views and ideas will enhance your learning and make you more successful in leadership. It also helps to show interest in what is important to those who work for you, or else you'll have a Sous Chef with renowned knife skills "accidently" cut himself to be sent home early because you refused to let him go like I saw someone do. There is always something to be learned in every situation, good, bad, and ugly. So get the lesson and keep on stepping.

As promised in the beginning of my apprenticeship, I did receive a couple of job offers. Every month the Chefs had their own meeting and the students had their own meeting and never the two mixed. However, during competition time we did work more with the Chefs and sometimes you would catch a Chef's eye, "What are you making now? $6.10? I'll give you $6.50." There were always students who would go for the 10, 15, or 30 cents more an hour. But, like I said, I had larger goals that went well beyond earning a few more pennies an hour.

I saw the difference between people who had this as a career versus people who had this as a job. For the ladies I first met in Garde-manger that was their job. That was not a career for them. That was just how they got their paycheck to make their living. But for the Sous Chef's this was a career. Well, for The Snake, it was a job that he fell into and not a career. I saw the difference, actually, we all did. But for the other Sous Chefs you could tell that it was a career because of the difference in their attitudes and what they were willing to do. Between that and seeing how things went in the classroom, I could see what the end game would be after graduation. I spent one more year at the Hyatt as not 3rd or 2nd, but 1st Pastry Cook before becoming the Executive Pastry Chef at the Hilton Head Island Hyatt Regency in 1986.

As I mentioned before when talking about my apprenticeship with the Hyatt Regency in Dallas, I learned to watch the leaders I came in contact with so that I could learn which leadership styles to imitate and which ones to avoid, and this was especially relevant to my first position as an Executive Pastry Chef. I remember a female Sous Chef who was brash and in your face. You can be assertive and to the point or you can be aggressive and a bitch. She was widely regarded as the later. She did have a lot to prove because I don't remember there being any other women who held her position at the time, and since she came to Dallas from New York I figured some of her attitude was a cultural difference in behavior, but whatever the reason no one in the kitchen ever called her "sweetheart." During my apprenticeship I never ended up working with her and I didn't have the opportunity to have a heart to heart about what it's like to be a Chef, I just knew that she was there and how she was perceived in the kitchen.

Don't get me wrong, I also met some great people during my apprenticeship, some of whom I am still in touch with. I had one co-worker who took me under her wings and showed me the ropes in our bakeshop, then allowed me to manager her when I was ready to step up. Mama Fay was old enough to be my mom and has since made her transition and is now in the sweet by and by. I learned a lot from Mama Fay and miss her gentle spirit still today. Working with and learning from Fay laid the foundation of how I treat new hires and staff; tough love and understanding works every time. She taught me how to keep my cool when all around are losing or lost theirs. This remains part of my managing style today.

I didn't know until years later after graduation that I was the first African-American female to graduate from the program in Dallas. I was very surprised when I found out. I would love to find out who the first African-American male was, but that had to be years before I started the program because if he was there the same time I was I'm sure we would have run into each other. Of course I knew that in my classes I was the only Black apprentice, but I never focused on it. There were other females in the program, but none were Black. It was never an issue for me because I put so much energy into trying to do well in the program. I was not the only one to overlook that piece of information at the time because the same person who brought it to my attention said "Yeah, we dropped the ball. We should have advertised you more, publicized you more."

Like I said before, I was never one to quit, so even when I stepped into the culinary arts program and realized that there was a lot more work involved in it than I originally though, I never once thought to quit. When I looked around my classes and didn't see another Black face, I never once thought to quit. When I saw how women were treated in the kitchen, I never once thought to quit. When a fellow female apprentice related the horrific story of her Chef telling her that a woman's place in the kitchen is on top of the table with her legs spread, I did not quit. My years as an apprentice really did show me what I was made of, and when I graduated from the program I realized that I may not have had all the same ingredients as everyone around me, but the mis en place that helped me get to that day were more than adequate to help me succeed. Now that I knew I had all the right ingredients I needed, it was time for me to figure out what I wanted to make of myself.

CHAPTER 3

Pre-heating

The first thing that any baking, broiling, or roasting recipe will do is tell you to pre-heat the oven. Pre-heating is the best way to be sure that you are cooking your dish correctly. In baking, a pre-heated oven ensures that you get the right chemical reaction you need for your yeast, baking powder, or baking soda to rise and give you the desired finishing effect. I refer to my early years as a professional in the kitchen as the pre-heating phase because I knew that my desired finish was to be an Executive Chef, and the early years in the kitchen definitely involved some interesting actions and reactions that helped me get there.

I graduated in 1984 but I didn't leave Texas until 1986 when I moved to Hilton Head, SC. When I first heard about Hilton Head I thought it was in Hawaii because it sounded like it should be the name of a Hawaiian island. When they told me it was in SC I just looked back at them with a blank look and asked, "Where am I going?" My boss David learned about the new Hyatt location in Hilton Head while attending a regional conference for property GM's. The Hyatt in Hilton Head was just upgraded from a Hyatt House, a hotel without an atrium, to a Hyatt Regency and was in need of a Pastry Chef. I also had the choice to move to Greenwich, Connecticut and be a Pastry Chef there, but I had no desire to leave the warm weather

I had become accustomed to and return to the cold in a place I didn't know and in a wealthy city that I knew I wouldn't be able to afford. Hilton Head is by no means a poor city, but Greenwich had a reputation for being one of the wealthiest cities in the nation. My years as an apprentice taught me how to make the most of a little bit of money, but I didn't want to be a stranger in a town where I would be both cold and poor.

In spite of all my efforts to choose the job that I thought would make me happy, I didn't enjoy Hilton Head. At the time, there was nothing in Hilton Head that I liked to do. During my time off in Dallas, I liked to get my hair and nails done, go shopping, hang out with the girls or play sports. I remember when Judy and I would go down to the Bahamas and stay for a couple of days. We had fun. There was shopping in Hilton Head but at those kind of prices I was not interested. And at that time, around '86 and '87, there were no malls or outlets. We had grass, farms, and a new bowling alley to entertain us when we you got tired of golf, the beach or tennis. It really didn't do much for me because I didn't like golf, the beach or tennis that much. There were also nightclubs, but I couldn't do that every night. I really didn't need that much techno music.

The shift from First Cook to Executive Pastry Chef was memorable, but not for the reasons most people would think. I got along ok with the two Black women who worked in the pastry kitchen with me-one was a well-travelled and cultured woman from Africa and the other was a South Carolina native. I put in a lot of hours in my new position, but this was not new for me because I was used to this. Dealing with the other managers was definitely new for me. We were not on the same page with each other and this became interesting in the small kitchen space we shared. There was a Swiss Executive Chef, a Sous Chef, a Restaurant Chef over the only fine dining restaurant in the hotel, there was someone else over the coffee shop, and there was me. We didn't have regularly scheduled meetings like I do in my kitchen now, but we did get together when there was an upcoming banquet with details that needed to be addressed. After being introduced to culinary politics in action I became grateful for not being required to be around the other managers any longer than I already had to.

It took me a while to adapt because I was not used to dealing with people who didn't have your best interest at heart. There were times when another Chef or manager would tell you to do something that they knew was wrong just so that they could set you up and make you look stupid. There were too many days when the kitchen "leadership" would butt heads and holler at each other and then go about their business. And then there were the behind the back maneuvers you had to look out for. Be on the look-out for the assistant food and beverage director who really has a culinary degree and thinks that she can do your job. When you were not around she would talk about how you plated your food incorrectly because that is not how she was taught to do it at her school and she is the authority on things like that. She would say anything to make her seem superior to you.

I am gratefully not aware of any particular instances with anyone trying to set me up, but in an environment like that you have to watch what's going on because you know that people are watching you and waiting to take advantage of you. There was one time when I scaled up a recipe because my cook needed a larger quantity than was originally recorded in the recipe, and I made a mistake in the math. So when she made it and it came out incorrectly she went hysterical. It didn't matter that I showed her how to fix the recipe, it was only cookie dough, but her face was red, she was embarrassed, and the situation was blown way out of proportion. Mistakes happen, but how you deal with them is the deal maker or breaker.

Hilton Head did leave me with some positive memories though. There was a Sous Chef we called Dutch. I just remember that he was from Utah and his parents were Dutch, hence the nickname. He told us that anytime he went on a job interview he would speak with his Dutch accent because it helped him "earn" a higher salary. It was memorable because he speaks English plain as day with no hint of an accent, but growing up with his parents he learned to mimic their Dutch accent. I have a girlfriend who did the same thing. Her mom is Australian and her dad is South African, so she naturally speaks the good Queen's proper English. You could always tell when she just got off the phone with her parents or just returned from spending time with them because her proper Queen's English would return. Back then so many people still had the mentality that European Chefs are better Chefs, so their accents were a plus during interviews. The public opinion about European Chefs being superior has been changing recently. To show you how slow this change is occurring, our own White House didn't have an American Executive Chef until 1994 when First Lady Hillary Clinton was impressed with Walter S. Scheib's cooking and invited him into the position. After Scheib left the position the White House got their first female Executive Chef when Cristeta Comerford took over the kitchen. She is also the first Chef of Asian descent.

The kitchen at the Hyatt in Hilton Head gave me enough memories by itself because it was so small! The main work table in the Dallas bake shop was about 6'x15' and all of our equipment was in the same room, but in Hilton Head my entire work space was about 7'x8' and we would have to go upstairs and down the hall to have access to a freezer. Compared to what I was used to in the 3 restaurant and 900 room Hyatt in Dallas, the newly upgraded 1 restaurant and 500 room Hyatt in Hilton Head was cramped.

I did have some interesting adventures in that little kitchen. I managed to talk the hotel into sending me to a marzipan modeling class in Maryland with a pastry purveyor. The 4 or 5 day classes cost about $1500 and then the hotel would have to pay for me to stay in a hotel. Not to mention that they had to feed me too. Marzipan is a mixture of ground almonds and sugar that forms a paste that can be molded into different shapes like modeling clay. As a Pastry Chef you always have to do some form of show piece work, it's required. I was already good at it, but I wanted the class to get better. As soon as I got back they found a way to get the money back that they invested in my trip by booking a party that required 500 pink panther marzipan figures. I had a month to finish them all in addition to my normal work load. Shaping and storing 500 pink panthers in a tiny kitchen was something else. I still get nauseated when I see the Pink Panther to this day.

As stressful as that was, I don't know if it compares to preparing for the Food and Beverage Director's wedding. The Food and Beverage Director was my boss's boss and of course it was my job to make the wedding cake. If that was not pressure enough, the wedding and the reception were on Daufuskie Island, which was a 30 minute trip to the marina, a 45 minute boat ride away to the island, and then transported to the reception location. Not to mention that all this was going to happen in the middle of the summer. At least for the banquet team, they could take raw food on the trip and prepare it on site. But for me, I needed to transport a cake with icing on it and hope that the 95 plus degree weather and humidity didn't melt the icing off of it. I already needed to be prepared to fix any bumps or nicks in the icing that resulted from travel. My plan was to freeze the three tier cake to help it survive the long trip, changing the ratio of butter to cream in the butter cream icing to lower the icing's melting point and raise its chance of surviving, and decided to transport it in tiers to avoid layering the cakes and inviting the opportunity for mayhem. I added the decorative fresh flowers on site. Fortunately, I didn't lose my job that day, so it must have worked.

In spite of all my Hilton Head adventures, I ended up leaving for Atlanta. At one point I moved off the island to live in Hardeeville with one of my co-workers. I should have known that wouldn't last long because a 45 minute commute each way on a one lane road was a high price to pay for a $12 or $13 a day salary. I just couldn't do that anymore.

When I moved to Atlanta I switched hotel chains and went from the Hyatt to the Hilton Atlanta & Towers. Although I was no longer the Executive Pastry Chef and took a position as an Assistant, I enjoyed being back in a larger kitchen as well as in the city again. It was interesting though because I never saw the skill level in the Executive Pastry Chef that I was used to seeing, like the skills I saw in Executive Pastry Chef who taught me during my apprenticeship. He managed the team and did all of the paperwork, but I never saw him doing centerpieces or showpieces. I'm not saying that he never made anything in the kitchen, but he was not the Pastry Chef I was groomed to be.

I got along pretty well with him, he was the first person I met who had to deal with employee alcohol abuse. Actually, it really wasn't the liquors or spirits that you are probably thinking. We had to lock up the vanilla extract because we had someone who would drink up to a pint of it every day with a cola. This was before vanilla cola was available in stores. It got so bad that we would go through a quart of vanilla in only two days. Everyone knew who it was but a good baker was hard to find, so we put up with the craziness for I while. There's always liquor in the pastry shop and they are usually kept under lock and key for obvious reasons. But this was the first time that we had to keep vanilla under lock and key.

I enjoyed the year I spent with them in Atlanta. I became good friends with the assistant. My brother was there in Atlanta too. I was still avoiding relationships because all I was interested in at the time was expanding my career and making some friends. I was not looking for anything. Until, of course, the Human Resource department of Grove Park gave me a call.

Grove Park Inn and Country club is a spectacular historic place located in the foothills of the Blue Ridge Mountains. I don't remember applying for a position at Grove Park so I had no idea how they got my name. Somebody must have passed it on. I had been kind of low key. I hadn't been active with any ACF Chapters so I was not participating in competitions to get anyone's attention. But when I got the call I agreed to go up for an interview. The director was Afro-American and a really good guy. I also met the Executive Chef. Two months after the interview I moved up to Grove Park and took the position as the Executive Pastry Chef and stayed there for five years. It did take me out of the city, but the opportunity was great, the money was alright, and the hotel was gorgeous with its mountain view in Asheville, NC.

One of my childhood friends said he thought Asheville was just a truck stop on the highway to get through the mountains. Having never been a truck driver or to Asheville, how he came up with that idea is still beyond me. I must admit that when the head-hunter first contacted me about this job, I thought he said Nashville. I too had never heard of or been to the area, so I took the 2 hour drive from Atlanta to the area and was enthralled with the beauty of the mountains. I had never been that close to them before and didn't grow up with them in my backyard. The closes things to mountains in Chicago are called John Hancock and the Sears skyscrapers! I saw my first waterfall, remembered to appreciate having four seasons, worked and produce more than I ever had, hosted a regional ACF conference, met my dear friend Barbra Johnson, married and became a mother in Asheville.

It was working at Grove Park that allowed me to utilize my skills in production. Organization, recipe conversions, multi-tasking, leadership, technical expertise, manual labor, and stamina are all part of the skills needed to get the job done right the first time. I had come to believe in the knowledge that it is always easier to scale down than it is to scale up. The intimidation or the feeling of being overwhelmed by the sheer volume of what needs to be done now, today, or this work week can make or break even the best cook. If your work background is that of employment in a high volume, fast paced kitchen where doing 250 covers, or dishes, a shift are the norm, then when you start working in a kitchen where the covers average 90 per shift, then it becomes a "piece of cake" to manage the production of the kitchen. There is no fear of not being able to keep up the pace and needs in the kitchen to produce the quality of their standards dictate.

However, if you reverse the situation and your new work environment demands you to keep a pace and standard that you have never done before, you have a great potential for failure and finding yourself "in the weeds." Being in the weeds is never an option!

There was definitely an increase of demand on my production skills when I moved to Grove Park. Our Sunday Brunch in the Blue Ridge dining Room averaged 600 covers, or dishes, and our major holiday brunches, like Mother's Day or Easter, would have as many as 2500 covers during a single shift. It helps that I was hired by a really good Chef who recognized and possessed himself great managerial and culinary skills.

Just like we did back in Dallas, at Grove Park we made everything ourselves from scratch. We made all the breads, cakes, pies, cookies, we made everything. It was helpful that I had a really good assistant who was a Culinary Institute of America graduate. We complimented each other quite nicely because his strength was in breads and, well, of course I could make breads but that was not what I wanted to spend my days doing. I also had a few morning bakers. One was the now retired Executive Pastry Chef who was working part time. He was from Yugoslavia, but if you asked him he would say, with his thick European accent, that he was from New Jersey. He had a lot of experience and skill to offer. I also had never seen someone eat so much butter! He slathered it on everything from a croissant sandwich for breakfast to a hard roll with a slice of pate. There were other men working with me, Jeff and Manuel.

Manny was from the Philippines and was very artisanal with breads before it was so popular in the states. Jeff was my part-time work horse. One of the few Afro-American cooks that I encountered who wanted to learn and progress in this profession. He was also working full time in a Biltmore club filling in as a savory and pastry cook. I can only hope that he used his skills and knowledge to his advantage. A great chef in the making who had knowledge of sweets and savory is one who would be in demand.

The Year before I started working there, the hotel shifted from being seasonal to year round. Grove Park would bring 40-50 Filipino men onto the property to help with the transition and to keep up with the busy high season. It was great because these men were world travelers and had a lot of experience to offer.

With the additional cooks, my staff would swell up to 15 -17 bakers and cooks. Three bakers and my assistant on the early morning or, "before air is up," shift as Barbra used to say. The AM crew of 3 or 4 cooks started punching in at 6AM, I would come in around 7 am, and there would be about 2 or 3 other people working the afternoon shift until the last event was done and all production was completed for the night. These numbers don't even include the interns and externs we would get from Johnson and Wales, Culinary Institute of America, and other local and regional culinary schools. There would always be someone in the kitchen working on something. Grove Park

Inn went from good, to this-is-crazy, to this-is-ridiculous in the 5 years I was there.

We had a high volume and fast paced kitchen that did about 600 covers a shift in Grove Park's one restaurant, the Blue Ridge Dining Room. "Cover" is a term for the traditional silver domes put over the entree plates of food as they leave the kitchen. So let's say that lunch service was open for three hours, then within that three hour period we served about 600 covers. That same restaurant hosts Friday night seafood buffets, Saturday night Prime Rib buffets, and Sunday brunch.

We would set up entire banquet tables of freshly prepared sweets and breads and rolls for each buffet. Counter tops displaying Challah, spinach and cheese, crusty French baguettes, rye and sour dough breads along with soft & hard rolls, poppy & sesame seeded rolls, caramelized onion focaccia and the signature Grove Park Inn lavosh were staples always on display. The dessert tables full of banana puddings, white chocolate mousse tortes, fruit trifles, German chocolate cakes, Charlotte Royales, chocolate mousse parfaits, fruit bavorois, Saint Honore Tortes, Tiramisu Torte, Pithiviers, carrot cakes, Frangipane slices enrobed in chocolate, eclairs, cream puffs and swans filled with fruit and vanilla whipped cream, pecan pies, apple strudels, all made from scratch were standards of the buffet. The action station of cherries jubilee or bananas foster prepared per order were treats enjoyed by many.

Our buffets became busier and our schedules became crazier. In the late 1980's, people were paying $28 per person plus the automatically added 15% gratuity to enjoy our buffets. Multiply that figure by the lowest count of 300 covers and you can see the profit margins were good and the servers were very happy!

While the buffets did make a big impact on our cooking volume that was not the only thing we did for the hotel. When you have catering or banquets, the pastry shop is the one department that has its hands on everything that happens. Be it continental breakfast, traditional breakfast, lunch, coffee break, or dinner, there's going to be a bread, dessert, or pastry in there somehow. Many kitchens try to cut costs by buying pie crusts or even entire pies, cakes, cookies, pastries and breads to save on paying salaries to workers in a pastry shop. But Grove Park understood that they could guarantee a higher and consistent level of quality by hiring and keeping the staff to make everything as needed. Besides, they would have been missing out on too much money for specialty events such as wedding cakes and company themed events requiring centerpieces and special amenities! Elvis Pressley themed parties requiring a replica of Graceland and some of his favorite foods, marzipan figures with chocolate truffles and petit fours for turn down service, cream & fruit filled wedding cakes with royal icing piped for décor. At that time, there was no place else to buy these quality and specialized items. All items were sold based on the skill level of the pastry chef and the team, so communication with the Sales & Catering Department was critical.

Grove Park had two large ballrooms in addition to all of the meeting rooms. Each time an addition or wing was added on to the original stone building a ballroom and banquet kitchen was added as well. We had drivers to deliver our pastry to the other side of the hotel as there was only one pastry shop. The driver would come up to the 9th floor where my shop was located to pick up the desserts for the Horizons and Sunset Terrace restaurants and for the Vanderbilt ballroom. Take them down to the loading dock and strap them in the back of the delivery truck to drive it up and down the hills to the other wing, I can't tell you how many times we had to re do items because the hills and bumps were too much or the driver was careless and too clumsy for the delicate pastry and desserts. One of my employees almost lost her job over the carelessness of the driver.

She was responsible for the production of the fine dining desserts in Horizons that day. One of the standards of upgraded service provided was giving house made butter roses with the bread service to each table. We would pipe 200 one-ounce butter roses daily and more on Friday & Saturday nights for the restaurant. When the driver was loading his truck with the order for Horizons, he struck the sheet pan with the butter roses on it with the plastic strips hanging in the doorway used to help keep flying insects out. The fragile butter roses were smashed and smeared all over the sheet pan and the plastic strips! Of course he was contrite on his accident with the roses, but that didn't help me or my staff as they now had to re do them for dinner service. The pastry cook was not happy as it was the end of her shift and the fact of re doing it because of his carelessness didn't sit well. After a little fussing and trash talking to the driver, she resigned herself to the task at hand. Luckily for us, we had become experts in piping them by then as we had done so many by that time. Within 30 minutes the driver was able to pick up the 2nd batch of butter roses and complete his tasks. Third times a charmer, right? Wrong! He dropped them again! Now I have a serious problem going on. It's almost time for the restaurant to open and they have yet to receive the butter roses for the night's service. The pastry cook is refusing to do them for a 3rd time and is packing up her tools to leave for the day. Having no time to properly counsel my employee, the choices I gave her were to help us get this done again so that the quality of service in the restaurant wouldn't suffer or to wait in the office so we could talk after the roses were done. She chose to wait and vent to the banquet chef about how she was being treated and how it was so unfair to be asked to do the roses again for the 3rd time. My PM cook and I knocked out the additional roses and I made the driver walk them over to the restaurant in the other wing. Horizon's restaurant opened on time and nobody was the wiser to the butter rose fiasco that happened in the back of the house. As for the employee who was ready to walk out on her job over piping butter roses, a counseling session with the executive chef and me straightened that out. The work can be exasperating and thankless at times, but there is never any good reason not to perform to the best of your abilities and to do the task assigned to you no matter how many times you are asked to repeat it. This is the difference between a professional cook wanting to be a chef and someone who has a job and is just there to get paid.

I had a large, beautiful shop but how much more could we possibly produce? This kitchen was much larger than the one in Dallas. I had three ovens, and one of them was a double-rack rotating oven that allowed me to cook twice as much in the same oven. The ovens helped us bake all of the breads we had to serve. We had wood counters and benches everywhere, we had great mixers, and the kitchen was just very well appointed. I had my own triple compartment sink and racks to do what I needed to do and didn't have to share it with the other areas. Usually you had to hide sheet pans and speed racks to finish production. There are never enough for each kitchen to utilize. Even my office was about three times the size of my entire workspace while I was in Hilton Head. For the most part, the equipment and the staff were great at Grove Park, but I left after five years and watching two burned out Executive Chefs come and go. I was burnt out and tired of not having a life of my own outside the shop. Now that I was a wife and a mother, this had become more important to me.

My husband was actually someone I had known from home. We met while in high school. He met my sister Judy first at the library when she was working there and they became instant friends. He lived across the tracks and on another side of town, and went to the all boy's private high school. He and Judy stayed in touch with each other despite the 3 year age difference and distance. There were a couple of times that he and I bumped into each other at house parties or Judy invited him over to our house. But it was actually her wedding almost 15 years later that brought us together. We ended up going out to discover the new Dallas night scene and talked all night long. He was recently divorced and had a precious little 3 year old daughter. We kept in touch over the next few months and he even came to visit me in my new mountain home. He and his daughter moved to Asheville and we got married a few years later in September 1993. I ended up leaving Grove Park in May 1994.

After Grove Park I went back to South Carolina and worked at the Omni Hotel, the crown jewel on the Charleston peninsula. Or at least that is what it was called before it was sold to another company and was renamed The Charleston Place Hotel. Again, I didn't go looking for the job at the hotel, some recruiter heard about me and called when a position opened up. My new assistant at Grove Park had actually come to Asheville from the Charleston Omni Hotel, so I did have the slight advantage of knowing a little history of what I was getting into. I'll also admit that one of the reasons I was looking forward to working for them is that this was another hotel chain where I would get hotel benefits and perks that would allow me to have free room accommodations at any hotel within the chain. I used to plan my vacations around the hotel chain! If there was not an Omni or Hyatt or a Hilton in the city where I wanted to go on vacation to, then plans would have to be revised. When we moved to Charleston and I took the job at Omni Hotel, I fully intended to stay there and raise my family there. We bought property in a quiet neighborhood and where there was a good school for our daughter. She was in the second grade by the time we moved.

While at the Omni, I found that I can still learn something on how to manage or not manage the team. Words can't adequately explain or express the style of management that I walked into. I worked with an English Executive Chef who I didn't see exercise his practical skills as a Chef. I'm familiar with the saying that 'if you don't know ask or surround yourself with people who do," and that's exactly what he did. He was also chauvinistic and racist and liked to keep mess going. At times he would try to be funny, but he was really coming off as racist and always at another's expense. I thought for a minute that it was the differences in the humor of the British versus that of Americans that kept up the rancor. As the only Black and female manager on staff, I caught on to his inappropriate comments. Learning to trust your gut and listen to the small voice in your head were all the signs needed. With a minimum crew of 20 cooks in the main kitchen, more than half were Black females who were constantly hearing and largely ignoring the Chef's rants and disparaging remarks. The Chef while speaking in subtle or not so subtle generalities "Well, we have got to cook that beef well done. This is a Black group coming in tonight for the banquet." Or when one of the pantry ladies had a health problem and passed out in the midst of plating up the dinner salad, the rest of the workers were instructed to step over her to get the meal plated on time. Hiring me then promoting a cook to be my salaried assistant without any input from me was the introduction to the craziness he liked to keep going.

The Chef's entire approach to food was totally different from what I was trained. A good example of this would be how he handled what I termed "The Jurassic Cake "issue. There was a downtown restaurant off of Market Street that was known for baking six and seven layer cakes and placing them in the windows to help draw in customers.

51

It didn't matter if the cake was dry or was made from a prefabricated mix. When you saw a huge cake like that, all it made you think about was going inside to eat cake! And with a single slice being six or seven layers, customers would always think that they were getting their money's worth. Well, when our Chef saw these cakes he decided that it would be a good idea for us to make cakes like it. I immediately objected to it and didn't want my name associated with it, but when the Executive Chef makes up his mind there is not much more that can be said.

Alongside the fine pastries and fine European styled desserts, which are known for being small and petite, we started serving these seven layer cakes. Our Chef wanted them served on the small dessert push carts. Soon after we began offering the cakes our servers started to complain about it. Their biggest complaint was that the large cakes were difficult to cut gracefully by the table side and serve because they would wobble. The slices couldn't even fit on a normal dessert plate and actually required the use of a full sized dinner plate. After receiving several complaints he finally gave it all up and let me, the Executive Pastry Chef he went out of his way to find and hire, do her job.

It also didn't help that I would have issues with one of his favorite people in the kitchen, who happened to be my new assistant. She had been in the kitchen for a long time and was dyslexic and didn't hesitate to remind you of it anytime she made a mistake on anything. I was told she used to milk the clock and get all of the over- time granted in that pay period. That stopped when she became a salaried employee! She was a culinary grad, but her methodology and some basic skills were missing. I know that I'm not perfect and that I don't know the science behind everything, but there are some basics that every culinary grad should know. That's why we are required to pass a practical cooking and written test before earning our certifications.

One day when I was off of work, she was having trouble with getting the egg whites for the meringue to tighten and fluff up to a stiff peak. Now an amateur may think that adding flour to it will stiffen the egg whites, but someone who went to culinary school for at least two years and has spent years in the pastry kitchen should know better.

This was not my assistant. The egg whites need to be pure so that they'll whip up to their highest volume, their highest peak. They will deflate if you add anything to them especially fat, and that's exactly what my assistant learned when she tried adding flour. Flour helps thicken a roux, not a meringue! Thankfully one of the crew came to her rescue and saved the day.

There was never much I could do because she was his favorite. It may or may not be coincidence, but I never actually met her before I accepted the job. She called in sick on the day I came for the interview, something I am told that didn't usually happen as she loved getting the over-time. However, when I decided to check out their work during Mother's Day brunch, which fell on the day before I began working and had the chance to meet most of the servers and kitchen staff anonymously I knew I had my work cut out. Being able to inspect and survey the order and details of the new work environment was a great opportunity to see what was going on in the kitchen before I got there. Even my daughter was not impressed.

I don't usually eat a lot of desserts, but I made sure I saved room for it that day. The meal itself was alright compared to all of the brunches I was used to eating at Grove Park, but the desert table was lacking. After I made sure my husband and daughter Bianca got their desserts, I watched Bianca struggle with cutting her cake. When I offered to help her I realized that the cake was still frozen. We were eating the brunch after 1 pm, and brunch usually starts around 11, and the cake was still frozen. After realizing that the kitchen overlooked serving a rock solid frozen cake, I started sampling everything else on the table to see what else they were up to. I later learned that they had a procedure where they would freeze cakes the night before they would be served, instead of wrapping them and putting them in the refrigerator. We had several issues, but that all ended when she left.

Our Food and Beverage Director took a position at The Peabody Hotel in Memphis and cleaned house. The Executive Steward was promoted to a higher position at that property, he took my assistant, and one other person from the catering staff. My Assistant went on to be the Assistant at The Peabody, she didn't go for a promotion but she did take a pay raise. As we started conducting interviews for her replacement, and for any cooks in my area, we started requiring them to bake something. I stopped relying on paper credentials to hire quality workers.

The majority of the people I worked with were always females. My head baker and my morning person, when I first started, were males but most of my staff was female. So the new Assistant I hired was a male, the decision was largely based on skill and in part was an effort to balance out my staff. I think it brings a whole new perspective. I like our differences too because it helps us make better decisions when trying to figure out what the best way is to handle different situations. I may see a situation one way and he will have his own perspective to offer. Everyone has their own ideas. And I don't want all women in my kitchen, nor do I want all men. And that's how I ran my kitchen for seven years before I left the Omni, which is now known as Charleston Place.

My son Brock was almost 3 years old when I left the Charleston Place. I wanted to be able to spend more time with him, and Bianca was already in high school. I wanted to be able to make dinner for my family and be home to eat it with them. Over the years, a group of us would get together and throw around different business ideas that would allow us to capitalize on our individual expertise. Unfortunately those lovely conversations were not associated with actions and we ended up watching our ideas become other people's realities. "We could open up a bridal shop and you could do the cakes…" was one of the ideas. Or, "we could open up a book store and you can have a little coffee snack shop or whatever." Of course we were talking about our version of Starbucks, a company that was not in our area at the time, but we never followed through on any of them. My husband and I went to a workshop with SCORE about how to write a business plan and attended multiple seminars and workshops geared towards starting a business, but nothing really took off just yet.

Instead of starting a business, I started exploring other directions for my career with teaching and television. During the summers of 1995 and 1996 I taught culinary classes at the local community college Trident Technical. The Charleston Naval Base had closed down and many of the base's former workforces enrolled at the technical college for retraining. So on top of my 50-60 hour work week I started teaching classes filled with students fresh out of high school and others who were fresh out of employment and were older than me. It was interesting to see though because even with the variety of life experiences, they were all on the same beginner level. I just taught one class that met twice a week for three hours a session. We needed more time because I was teaching them to make doughs, batters and everything else from scratch, bake and cool it and then decorate and serve it.

It was my first time teaching in a classroom setting, but it never really made me nervous. The course syllabus and textbook was provided, so I started designing the lesson plans from there. Since I know that hands-on experience helps, I would bring in some of the people I worked with to talk about different techniques we covered and to do demos to help the students. It worked out great. I had to think of tests that would actually test their knowledge instead of just relying on true/false and multiple choice guessing tests. It made me open up some books myself to remind me of why I did some of the things that had already become second nature to me.

I liked the teaching experience. I would try my best to set it up where I would be off the day after the classes because the teaching days would be long days. After teaching for a while, the dean invited me to be on an advisory committee to determine what the community needed and how to expand and best meet the community's needs. We were trying to find out how to best utilize a newly purchased space next to the main campus. We met quarterly until we made our decision, and now part of that new space is an expanded location for the school's culinary arts program. The last time I taught, in 2008, was actually in that new location.

I also taught at Johnson and Wales, when it was open in Charleston. It was an intense nine day session from 4 pm to 11 pm with entry level culinary students trying to grasp baking and pastry basics. Most of them did okay, and the ones with previous experience did even better, but you can only teach so much each day with 9 different topics to cover each day. It's especially tough with a group who is fresh in the field and most of them are interested in becoming savory, not pastry students. It dampens their motivation to learn and excel a little, but for the most part, they still did ok. They needed to pass the class to move on with their studies. And with every class there is one or two who is demanding the "A," even if they didn't earn it. They got A's in high school so of course they should get them in college right? Wrong! Oh the agony of defeat and loss of the 4.0 GPA.

Teaching was something that just sort of happened, and my first time on television really was a fluke as well. It was not anything I was politicking for, but there was another Chef, a friend of mine who was on the local CBS program called "Coffee With". The national morning show would break away to the 4 minute local cooking segment that rotated three different Chefs on Fridays. One of the Chefs dropped out, so my friend gave them my name and the producer called me. I turned her down flat. I told her that I was too busy and wouldn't be able to get away. I talked to my Executive Chef about it and told him my response and he told me to do it. It would be good to see the reaction from the other Executive Chef who was always in the limelight. Steal some of his thunder was his plan. My chef never saw it as an opportunity for me to advance and advertise our business or my career, just a way to thumb his nose at someone else.

I would arrive at 7:45 am for the 8:35 am show and would have the opportunity to talk with the crew and news anchors while setting up for the segment. The kitchen set had no running water so when I needed it, I had to leave the studio and find a water fountain or the bathroom sink to fill up a pot or pan. They loved it the first time I did it and they invited me back again. That was the year I was pregnant with my son Brock, so it was interesting that just about every time I was on the show my Chef's jacket was getting bigger than the one I wore on my previous appearance. Having people watch me while I worked never bothered me. Once you know it's your time and that red light that tells you it's live on the cameras comes on, knowing what I was doing and having experience in it made all the difference in the world. Also having an engaging host helped too. I was not really camera shy, I just wanted to make sure that everything was done right and that the end results on the plate was up to my standards.

It was an unpaid opportunity that I enjoyed. It would take at least 1 to 2 hours of prep to set myself up for the 4 minute segment. Everything had to be done in duplicate and in different stages of preparation. Food and dishes, pots and pans, tools and equipment had to be packed for the drive across town. Who knew that the same little girl who loved to watch Julia Childs and the Galloping Gourmet would end up in her own 4 minute cooking segment? It's not the same as having your own one hour show each week, but it was still something that I would have never guessed that I would have the opportunity to do while I was an apprentice. I used recipes on the show that I used all the time at Charleston Place and Grove Park. I did get a little more press from being on the television. There were articles in the local newspaper and other trade magazines. Between the show and the articles, it was interesting to have strangers walk up to me while I was out and about in town and tell me where they saw or read about me. But after a year and a half the station changed formats and stopped running the show. No I didn't receive a paycheck from the "Coffee With" cooking segment, I got rewarded with the exposure, free press and networking opportunities.

The experiences of teaching in a culinary arts program and cooking on a local cooking segment gave me great insights on different career paths. I didn't want to be the chef who stayed too long in the kitchen; the dinosaur that couldn't keep up or be on that ever-changing cutting edge. Working in a hot kitchen 5 or 6 days a week, 10 to 12 or more hours a day on a concrete floor will take its toll on anyone. Working weekends, nights, and holidays was not how I wanted to spend the rest of my career. My daughter was raised with me working this kind of schedule, but her brother, who is 12 years younger, would be raised with a different reality I determined.

A serious conversation over wine and dinner with my specialty foods sales rep shifted my focus and changed my course. We decided to combine our expertise and form our own distribution company. Focusing primarily on baking and pastry items, because it was our strength, we would be able to fill a void in what was recognized as a foodie town, Charleston, South Carolina.

CHAPTER 4

Prepping, The beauty of it

Some people don't have a clue what they want out of life, they just keep moving along and try to make the best decision they can under any given circumstances. Others have a vague idea of their future goals and then take, or even make, opportunities over time that will edge them towards those goals. I guess I'm more in that second group because when I went into my culinary apprenticeship years ago, I never once thought about starting my own business. Then again, maybe I shouldn't be so surprised because I was raised with the idea and spirit of making things happen for yourself. If it is to be, it is up to me. So apparently, owning my own business was to be.

I never wanted to own a restaurant because I didn't want to work at night and the statistics were seemingly stacked against you being successful. This was when fine dining restaurants made the most money and had the highest overhead. A bistro during the day to serve breakfast and lunch might have worked well though. During my earlier days at the Omni, I remember telling my Chef that I would rather have more time off then the 3% tax increase called a raise. He didn't understand the statement at the time, but even then I knew that my freedom to do what I wanted with my personal time was more important to me than the additional tax burden associated with a pay raise. You can get more money, but when time is up, it's gone. You never get it back.

It took 2-3 months to put the business plan for Food Fetish together. Food Fetish was a wholesale specialty food distribution company that primarily focused on raw ingredients and other pastry products. It took us another couple of months to get the money we needed. Everyone kept telling us that our success happened quickly. To us it felt like it was taking forever because we were passionate about our vision but we kept running into so many people who kept telling us "no."

Some of the biggest objections to our plans were from people who wanted us to put more of our own money into it. Others thought that we needed more experience in the business already. I didn't understand the request for us to put more money into it because, the way I saw it, if I had all that money to begin with I wouldn't have had to ask them for it! The bank wanted real estate for collateral. I did have a house at the time, but the partner didn't have anything to put up for collateral because she lived in an apartment. But her parents owned two homes and my sister had property in Texas that she and her husband offered up as collateral. The bank chose the local home over my sisters'. Finally, someone gave us the "yes" we needed.

We found our warehouse by accident. We were out to lunch one day and just happened to look in the classified section to find a 4,000 square foot warehouse. We had looked at warehouses before this one, but in spite of their prime location we often ran into logistical issues like having a big oak tree in the middle of the driveway/loading dock. How were our delivery trucks supposed to be able to get in and out of the docks with a tree in the middle? We had our eye on another facility at the time, it had an air conditioned warehouse, an expensive lease, and a 30-page leasing agreement that required us to contact the owner if we wanted to do almost anything, including mounting a picture to the wall. So when we found the Ashley River warehouse with the space we needed plus room to grow that was right off of both interstates and met the retired woman who owned the property, I started drafting my letter of resignation to Charleston Place.

I gave my notice in June 2001 and Food Fetish, Incorporated was born. To make things more interesting and challenging, while we were drafting our business plan and searching for our warehouse, a DC based food distribution company opened a satellite office in Charleston. So we opened up having a price war with the competitor. Fortunately, we had the advantage of having a Chef on staff, yours truly who was available to consult and demonstrate the products and being able to focus on providing excellent customer service. For example, we would allow a customer to buy an 11 pound block of chocolate versus the 55 pound case. Instead of forcing them to buy a full case, scrambling to find space to store everything and have their money tied up in product sitting on a shelf.

Knowing the product helped me talk with other Chefs and clients better than the average sales person, and explaining how using the services we at Food Fetish provided would benefit their kitchens was a great marketing plan. The partner was the sales person, because of her previous experience with a specialty food distribution company, but my experience with using the products helped seal the deals. It was amazing how many Chefs and restaurant owners didn't know much about their own pastry programs and products they already had in place, so an emphasis on quality and usage was a big selling point. Executive Chefs as well as the Pastry Chef were our main clients. It was good that they knew they could call us for technical, pastry, and baking concerns as well as delivering the forgotten must-have-it-now-product at the last minute. We shipped and sold our products throughout South Carolina, North Carolina, Coastal Georgia, and Northern Florida. I might go to restaurants to review their menu and show them how to upscale, upgrade or just better utilize what they had, but somebody had to be in the warehouse for shipping and receiving. Learning how to operate our second-hand forklift was not a class I had in culinary school! Yet loading and unloading pallets became part of my routine.

When I started Food Fetish, I changed from being the person who used to pay the husband and daughter to do the typing of newsletters or anything else that involved working on a computer every day. I even won a computer at one of the ACF conferences and I gave that one to my husband to help him manage the household finances and everything else that people were doing on computers at that time.

Now I handled the bookkeeping, phones, and logistics, including shipping and receiving and inventory. We had an accountant who came in quarterly to do taxes and I signed off on them. I also managed the semi-annual inspections from the USDA. It was always an unannounced visit, and it was usually a three hour event. The first hour was coffee and talking and the rest of the time was spent inspecting the facility and making sure we were storing and handling the food correctly. If I was not ready, I was not answering the door. There were a couple of times I thought to myself, "I got out of the kitchen to do what?" But working at the Fetish was the 8-4 Monday thru Friday day job that I wanted so that I could spend more quality time with my children.

It was a great learning experience working with bankers, growing a customer base and my business. Securing a lease for the warehouse was an experience in and of itself. It also helped to see just how a business could and should operate.

From the beginning, business ramped up fast. A local business development program provided assistance with managing our growth, and the director did a great job of explaining different things we could do to improve the flow of the work duties and how to handle clients. We decided to participate in trade shows by doing presentations featuring our products; this would bring publicity for both our vendors and Food Fetish as the company who would provide the product. I also enjoyed them because now that I no longer worked in a kitchen, doing cooking demonstrations and competitions were the best way to keep my skills sharp and give me first-hand knowledge of new products and equipment as they became available.

One of the first trade shows Food Fetish, Inc. was scheduled to participate in was in Las Vegas, Nevada. We were going to share a booth and get some information to help us become more successful. Unfortunately, our plane was grounded in Memphis before we could arrive at our Vegas destination. There was no way of knowing that September 11, 2001 would be a bad day to fly.

By the time news of the attacks on the World Trade Center and the Pentagon spread, we were on the connecting flight from Atlanta and they turned us around and put us down in Memphis. No one gave us any information about what was going on until we landed on the ground. All of the televisions in the terminal were off with the exception of one television in a bar. As I watched the news coverage I just kept thinking that I was watching a promotional movie trailer, so you can imagine my shock when I learned that this was not a movie. This was real and we were stuck in an airport that was 12 hours of driving away from home. I quickly decided that we needed to get out of the airport and to a hotel. It was chaos in the baggage claim area as everyone was trying to do likewise, find a hotel, get a rental car or even inquire about another flight! Luckily I was in arms reach of some man who was on a hotel phone getting his room reserved when he yelled out "they have rooms left at the Holiday Inn!" I grabbed that phone and got a room booked and shuttle service to the hotel.

We were all dazed and in total disbelief of the day's events. They really needed to open that lobby bar!

My sister Judy was stationed in Arlington, VA and at times worked in the Pentagon. I began to get worried about her as I couldn't get through to her on the phones. Calls were not going thru to DC. That night while we tried to sleep, I was more worried about my sister Judy who was still in the military than I was about how I was going to get home from Memphis. It was around midnight when I finally thought to have my husband check the emails. An email message from her telling us that she was safe and on lock down was there the whole time. My sister Cheryl and her daughter Kyra drove from Atlanta the next morning to pick us up and my husband and kids drove us home from Atlanta later in the day. Talk about a caravan of love. God is good.

Everything worked out for me and my family after September 11th, but it was getting ugly for Food Fetish. Businesses practically stopped for 3 months because no one traveled for the rest of the year and all of the groups that had plans and businesses that booked hotels and conference services cancelled. Fortunately, it didn't stay like this for long. With the new year came travel, conventions and tourist. Our business began to grow so fast that our receivables couldn't keep up. With customers from her previous job and I with the ACF Chefs and other Chefs I knew in the industry, we had a good client list to grow from.

People wanted our business but some were slow to pay. It didn't help that most of our vendors expected their money within 15 days of providing products and our biggest customers who we sold the most to had 30 day terms for payment. It was even worse when we had clients on a 15 day term that didn't pay until 30 days after. It may work when you have smaller quantities and you have to come out of pocket to pay vendors and wait on clients to return the money, but our business was ramping up and that proved to be a lot of trouble. At this rate, some vendors would start requiring us to pay cash on delivery.

After the first 18 months or so, Food Fetish finally hired a part-time employee to deliver orders locally on Mondays, Wednesdays, and Fridays. My background in the kitchen helped me to prepare for interviewing the person we hired. Our newspaper advertisement always generated a good turnout. We got a lot of feedback. I interviewed paralegals, nursing assistants, realtors, and people with all kinds of degrees looking for a part-time job. It was a sure sign that things were changing in the economy. Everyone was very interested in a 20 hour a week $10 an hour job with no benefits other than an occasional bag of free chocolate and reimbursed mileage. I always chose somebody who needed a job and not the professional individual who just wanted something else to do while waiting for the job market to change.

Hiring a part time delivery person allowed us to do more and seemed to work out much better. There would be times that semi-trucks would arrive after the sun went down and the outside lights on the building were temperamental, so we would turn our cars towards the back of the truck's trailer and unload pallets of frozen danishes and croissants by headlights. This was one of many times I would work up a sweat inside a freezer with a temperature reading of -10 degrees Fahrenheit.

My husband and I separated in 2002 and eventually divorced. Brock was not in school yet when his father left, but I could tell that he was missing him. So we worked it out whereas to the fact that Brock would spend his summers with his father and stay with me during the school year. The business didn't have anything to do with my divorce, but the change in the family life influenced my decision years later to leave Fetish.

The one thing I learned about being in a business is that there can't be a 50/50 split on decision making because somebody has to be able to make the final call. That was definitely part of our problem. She would say right and, sure enough, I would say left. It didn't matter what it was, we just didn't see how to handle business the same way. We were really stuck on stupid! So then what could you do? You couldn't make every decision with 50/50 split in power. Somebody is going to get upset. No one told us that when we were setting up our business and filling out our corporation papers. I learned that there should be a 49/51 split or at least another person or entity to break the ties.

My business partner was in charge of outside sales. She was the person customers would meet when they contacted our company. She would be the one to make the trips throughout the Carolinas, coastal Georgia and northern Florida to go see them. I eventually had the one part-time employee to help me manage everything. Although being able to spend time with my children was part of my motivation for leaving the kitchen and starting the business to begin with, it was even more important for me now because I was now divorced and I had both our son and daughter with me. As a single mother, I needed to have flexibility in my work schedule.

It's interesting that at the start of our business everyone was turning down our loan and investment requests because they wanted us to put more of our own money into it, and not one of them addressed the one issue that was the biggest contributor to our struggle as a business-our decision making process. Most people would assume that we would have had problems with getting clients, but that was never our issue. We were really well suited for the whole thing, it was just the decision making standoffs that got in the way. It really didn't help when vindictive games came into play, "Okay, well...she did this so I'm gonna do this." Tit for tat just doesn't work.

We started Food Fetish in July 2001 and I left in October 2009 after a series of major disagreements. I was on my way to what I was missing. Being creative in the kitchen full time!

I officially formed Culinary Concepts, LLC. As I said, I was always cooking for friend's dinners, parties, and weddings, so I decided to use my business experience from Food Fetish to promote what Food Fetish didn't allow me to do, cook. Culinary Concepts is more than a catering business, I created experiences with food. After years in the kitchen of high end hotels and eight years of helping restaurant owners find ways to upgrade their menus while using the same foods they already have in the kitchen, I wanted to put it use in my own business. The good thing is that this business didn't require financial backing; it was just about advertising and getting started. It would be as much as I wanted to make it.

I prefer to do smaller parties now, just because it's a lot easier and I can focus more on the details. You can do so much nicer work with smaller numbers. I recently had two catering jobs in one day, one was for a lunch group of 80 people and then there was dinner party of 7. Although there were only 7 people in the dinner party, there was still a lot of prep. I had help with shopping for the lunch group, but I was the one woman prep, cook, serve, and cleaning party for the dinner group.

I couldn't even tell you who the first person was that I catered for through Culinary Concepts, LLC because I have been cooking for people all the while. The events start to run into each other. But one of the things I love doing the most through Culinary Concepts, LLC is food demonstrations where I have the chance to introduce people to new foods or at least cook the foods they already love in ways new to them. Healthy cooking demonstrations that I did for the American Cancer Society, South Carolina Department of Health and Environmental Control, SC Women Infants and Children, Imara Magazine, The Tri-County Black Nurses Association, Palmetto Project, gave our state some much needed help with keeping and maintaining optimum health initiatives. I once did a presentation where I prepared the food and then talked about nutrition and the different spice and flavors that was layered in the food. One of the participants immediately commented about how he didn't like the way brown rice tasted. The irony is that he was telling me this while he was downing a dish with brown rice in it, he just didn't recognize it because of the way I prepared it. I always explain that good nutrition does not have to be expensive. You buy seasonal, you buy local, and you cook it properly, and it's good. So many people have preconceived notions about what they like or don't like and have not even tried half of the foods. If you try eating foods with different flavors and seasonings you will be surprised with how it turns out. There is always something new you can introduce to yourself and family. Be it cuisines from around the globe or something as simple as an additional herb and spice can make all the difference in the variety at the table.

I want to do more teaching and demonstrations to show people how to prepare the foods they want to eat but to eat them in a healthier way. I also like introducing people to super "new" foods like couscous and quinoa. I like teaching cooking methods to the public that embrace methods like braising and the art of sautéing. Other procedures that can liven up menus and lead to eating healthier to a southern culture that favors frying, deep-frying, and even re-frying foods like chicken, Twinkies, and butter!

There was a business out in Hollywood, SC that had amazing pecan wood smoked salmon that I used to feature in my catering events. The owner built his own five foot plus long smoker with rotating shelves. He also smoked prime rib, duck, oysters and a lot of other foods too. I first met him while I was still working at the Fetish. We were looking to expand beyond only providing pastry foods and I thought the product was excellent and had a lot of potential. But my partner was not as enthusiastic about it as I was, and if the salesperson didn't like it there was no way that we could do business with him because it wouldn't be properly promoted as the love and understanding of the product was not there. As the saying goes, "you can't fake the funk!"

By the time I left Food Fetish and he and I talked about being business partners although he had already closed the smokehouse. Hollywood is a small rural town with a population of only a few thousand. Not many people in small rural areas buy enough pecan smoked salmon to keep a business like this open. I and a friend of mine, who had sampled and feasted on the smoked delicacies, got him to open up again for the upcoming holiday season by promising a certain amount of business. He opened up his kitchen and everyone was happy. I made sure I bought enough salmon to fill my freezer in case he didn't stay open.

Even with my background in food distribution get backing for it. However, during one of the several presentations I made to potential investors, I met a Charlestonian who knew just about everyone, and he has made a big impact on my career and my life.

Lee Moultrie was the last person to arrive to the Smokehouse presentation. A mutual friend told me that Lee was a true go getter and that I would need to have my act together. I was not worried about it because I had my act together, that's what I always strive to do. So I presented a meal featuring the pecan smoked salmon and my business plan and financial statements. Soon Lee started asking several questions. I answered several questions. Then he came up with more questions. That night, we both left with a light bulb blinking and having an "ah ha" moment.

I may not have gotten the financial backing I was seeking during those presentations, I instead received something better. I met somebody who would speak for me when I couldn't, somebody who opened doors when I couldn't, somebody who could see things that I did not. I was given a mentor and a business partnership was born.

We used to meet at a coffee or sandwich shop all the time and brain storm ideas. Lee was not in the culinary business although he had front of the house experience. We would be trying to piece together the puzzle of my life experiences with his connections in the healthcare arena. How could we best utilize my 25 years of expertise with the current culinary and healthcare trends to help our communities was our goal. Those sessions could be so intense and provoking at times. I was not use to talking about myself, answering questions about my career choices or discussing future plans. I was learning almost as much as Lee. Sometimes you take for granted what you know or maybe you just don't know how to celebrate or advertise your knowledge and expertise.

He almost fell out of his chair when he learned that I was the only Black, Certified Executive Pastry Chef in SC, one of only 7 Certified ACF Examiners in the state. And the only Black female Executive Chef inducted into the ACF's honor society, American Academy of Chefs living right here in Charleston.

Lee has been a great sounding board for Culinary Concepts, LLC and with everything else that he does in the community he has been great at getting the word out about it. It was not long before Lee took on the role of my business development manager. Game changer indeed!

CHAPTER 5

Turning up the Heat

I have gone from being a little girl who cooked as part of her household chores, to being a waitress at a hotel who was curious about cooking, to convincing a Chef that he was not wasting his time by teaching me pastry and baking techniques, to being an Executive Chef, teaching, doing a local television show and starting my own business. At face value it might look like I've done everything you can do with a culinary degree, but not quite. I was always told that corporate is the place to be if you want to be a Chef.

May 2010 I started working at a local hospital as Executive Chef. In March of the same year the hospital hired Sodexo to manage the kitchen and Sodexo started advertising the position. I was already friends with a Sodexo Director and other hospital Chefs, and they encouraged me to apply.

As the Executive Chef over the hospital's kitchen, this job I was told was supposed to be a lot more administrative. There are systems that I have to put in place to make everyone's job easier and to better track the nutritional values, monies spent and food safety. In a perfect world, being able to complete these tasks daily while training staff, cooking meals, attending meetings and following all of the guidelines set by both companies would make for a great food and nutrition department. The systems work when given the time and tools and resources to implement them.

What I like about working at the hospital is that what we do is about serving the patients. The hospital food is one of the main things everyone talks about when they go to a hospital. It's amazing to me when you get the complaint, "well, my vegetables were still raw." No they were not, they were just not overcooked and limp like so many people do when they cook at home. Broccoli is supposed to be green and not yellow. There's supposed to be a little bit of crisp and crunch when you chew on a piece of green bean. It's not supposed to melt on your tongue and just swallowed. Too many people are missing the nutrients we need. I'm sure that if more people would eat to live instead of living to eat there would be fewer people in the hospital. I see orders come in the kitchen for patients requesting pancakes, cinnamon rolls and four pieces of bacon for breakfast. The other day someone order chili mac with sides of rice and navy beans. Starch, starch, and more starch. We are supposed to be making people better, but we can only do so much when the same bad habits and lifestyles still exist. I have heard some doctors refer to this as job security!

Lee talked me into joining with Toastmasters around August 2011. We agreed that working on my public speaking abilities would help me during demonstrations and other opportunities. I did 1 and sometimes 2 speeches a week to become a Certified Communicator. There must be 10 speeches given for this certification, and while some people take a year for this, I had it in 3 months.

I still attend meetings on Friday nights. I am currently the VP of Education, setting the agenda and trying to help everyone reach their goals. I like being a Toast Master, it's been very helpful. It's not just about being comfortable with public speaking, it's also about leadership. For example, we did a session on listening. We would have to listen to someone speak and try to paraphrase the different things that we heard. There is always room for improvement, I'm not there yet. My goal is to get better at communicating along the way.

I hate to admit it, but Lee was right about Toastmasters opening up other opportunities. One of the ladies I ran into at Toastmaster was a sales person for a company I knew through Food Fetish, and she now works with a local food bank. The food bank has a kitchen there now, and I am looking forward to leading their clientsin some training sessions.

December 2011 I started doing a cooking segment with "LowCountry Live" a local ABC television morning show. Lee met one of the morning anchors by chance in a grocery store parking lot and made the connection. I use the term "met" loosely as we were about to sit down for one of the many coffee breaks/meetings when he looked up and saw Laura riding by. Dashing out of the coffee shop with our business cards in hand, he made the most out of the opportunity. Laura made sure the contact and shared information made its way to the appropriate people at the tv station, and they called a few weeks later to offer a 4 minute spot. We jumped on it immediately. The "LCL" crew has been like family. I have been supported and given access to other opportunities not afforded to all.

I also stay active with the World Association of Chefs Society (WACS). It's the international association of Chefs with about 90 Million members worldwide. As an ACF member, I am automatically a member with WACS. Because WACS recognizes the issue with having women becoming Chefs, there is a group called Women in WACS and I reached out to the current President who is from Poland to see how I can help. WACS offers help by training and mentoring to different countries that want and ask for help. There is a train the trainer program that I have signed up for that would allow me to go abroad and help other culinary students learn more about their profession. I do believe in giving back as I was afforded the same courtesy in my apprenticeship and it really feels good to do so.

One thing I have not done in a while but would like to when I have time is to go back to examining and proctoring practical test on Cruise Lines. In 2008 I became an ACE, Approved Culinary Examiner for the purpose of helping cooks, educators and chefs become certified on the level of expertise they seek. It was just before Christmas break 2008 when I learned of the opportunity to be an examiner on board a cruise line. One of the Chefs at the technical college was also an examiner and was preparing to go on his first cruising exam. Upon

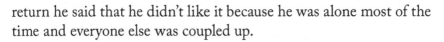

return he said that he didn't like it because he was alone most of the time and everyone else was coupled up.

My first cruise was a 7 day cruise then 4 days out followed by another 3 days out on 2 different ships in Los Angeles, California to ports in Mexico. Both were on the Royal Caribbean cruise line, the only cruise line that certifies their cooks and chefs. There is a standard test for everyone in ACF worldwide, but they have to be ready for them. I went to observe and record the progress of the training given to them by RCCL's corporate chefs, see new places, eat different cuisines and make some new connections. I had been examining stateside, but this was my opportunity to examine internationally. Fly to England to take a cruise to Ireland or setting sail from the Florida coast to the Caribbean was an adventure to be had.

We finally proctored an exam for a Certified Pastry Cook and one for a Certified Executive Pastry Chef on RCCL. The CEPC is a 4 hour exam. You have to decorate 2 cakes, one iced and one glazed. The cakes should be already baked, you just have to fill and ice them. You have to make a yeast dough, make four different types of rolls, one dozen each from that dough. You must prepare and plate 4 cold and 4 hot desserts. You must work according to health and safety guidelines and any food safety issues can mean failing automatically. It's all graded by a point system, the things that you do or oversee as a pastry chef every day is what is graded. It's a very specific test, a lot of people don't understand the pastry part of it until they actually see it. 4 hours is the longest time given of all of the practical tests, after seeing all of the requirements, that time really does go by quickly.

Chapter 6

Mignondise

What I would like to say is thank you sincerely to all of the chefs and people I have worked with who have made me what I am today. An Executive Chef, a Certified Executive Pastry Chef (CEPC), Approved Culinarian Examiner (ACE), Certified Culinary Administrator(CCA), entrepreneur, an inspirational speaker and to date the only African-American female Chef in the honor society of the American Culinary Federation, the American Academy of Chefs (AAC).

The journey was never that easy but it was also never that hard. I always found it amazing or maybe interesting that my fellow students, coworkers could spend all their money on the next night out, the next round of drinks or the next big event in town, but couldn't spend their money for their own education, go to a seminar or conference or convention. They wouldn't spend the money on their own tools, equipment, books or uniforms. Choices made for the moment or for the moments after. Do you spend the five dollars now or do you take the five dollars and invest in your future?

I didn't really have a mentor. It was something that was never even discussed when I was in culinary school. And truth be told I am not sure I wouldn't have known what to do with one who offered to be that for me. I was not used to talking to other people about my problems, career, issues or concerns. I had my family, my sisters and brother to discuss with. Sharing the journey of my successes and my failures was key to gaining wisdom and knowledge and keeping my sanity. I truly wish that my father had been able to better prepare me for the work force and the men that I encountered in it. It was something that was not discussed with me by my parents. So I hope that by writing this, the ladies especially will know that it's not impossible to achieve whatever level of success you dare to dream or conceive. You just have to go for it. Do it.

Dysfunctional families, lack of money, lack of support, lack of guidance should not be used as an excuse not to succeed. Life is full of peaks and valleys, everybody always wants more money, we all need a hand up, sometimes even a hand out, and the light to guide our way. Getting knowledge and information today is so much easier than when I was in school. Everything is a click or stroke away. Learning how to use the tools that God gave you, listening to that inner voice is key to your success. Sometimes you have to be the trailblazer and take the road less traveled. The Internet, computers, smart phones, software applications make it impossible for you not to become aware and informed on your chosen path. "If it is to be it is up to me" is a song that we used to sing in Sunday school. Those words of positive reinforcement and others that were preached, taught, and sung to me or by me, gave me the motivation and the courage and conviction to go forth to be successful. "I am that I am," something that was quoted and discussed about in our youth classes in church as well.

I grew up with strong, positive influential women in my daily life. The church, my mother, my aunt's all played a part in my upbringing and how I looked at life. It is so true that you get out what you put in. So if you're constantly told you will never amount to anything, you are stupid, you can't do it and you believe it, then chances are you will make it come true. But if you are told you can do it, you are God's whole and perfect child, that you are somebody, that you are young, gifted and bright then chances are you will make that your reality.

The rest of my story is still being written, so don't count me out. When I see more women and chefs of color in leadership roles I know we are in a better place. To have diversity and inclusion in any

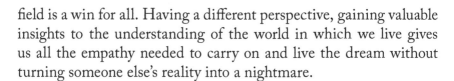

field is a win for all. Having a different perspective, gaining valuable insights to the understanding of the world in which we live gives us all the empathy needed to carry on and live the dream without turning someone else's reality into a nightmare.

Please have patience with me for I am not done yet. The statistics have to change to reflect inclusion. The faces of the Executive Chef and the Executive Pastry Chef have to be that of the world's rainbow. The opportunities afforded to one must be given to all. My toque is put on the same as a man, why am I not treated the same and given the same opportunities?

During one of the many brain storming sessions the information of the lack of minorities in the kitchens in leadership roles came up. Reports were being written in magazines and talked about on television. Where are all of the Black Chefs? What happens to all of the females in culinary schools? "Can you name 5 Black Executive Chefs who are leading a restaurant?" Sadly I couldn't. Sure I know educators who are on the executive level, but I was hard pressed to name more than 3 Black Executive Chefs. That is pretty sad commentary in an area in which minorities have always worked and made their living in.

We need to wake up, step up and make it happen. Go get what is rightfully yours to have once you have prepared yourself, put in the time to get the experience and qualifications. Don't just sit on the sidelines hoping to get noticed or included. One student I met at a conference was upset and in tears after attending a networking breakfast with the Senor Chefs. She was ignored by the Senor Chef while they were seated having breakfast. The attention of the Chef was divided between the White student cooks seated at the table. Her complaint was that of discrimination. My first question to her was what did she do to interject herself in the conversation? Did she introduce herself? Did she speak up and out at all? Her response was "No" to all the questions. Yes that Senor Chef didn't respond correctly, but the student didn't either. Ultimately it was more of her loss as she was the one who had the most to gain from the experience and she did nothing to help herself.

Here are my tips to aspiring chefs: (1) record what you are doing, (2) keep in touch with the people you meet, (3) stay active in your local ACF Chapter, and (4) stay open-minded and ready to receive.

1. Write down, record, and take pictures of what you are doing because, believe it or not, one day you're going to forget the details of what happened, what you did and where you were. As I go through my notes and pictures I realize now just how much of my experience I have forgotten. As an apprentice we were required to write down and make a picture of one item we did each week to have a three year journal. I've never been one for journaling, even when it was require. Most of us, back in the day for that journal, would spend the last month or two catching up because they didn't look at it. It's a lot easier these days with digital cameras on most of our phones. Write down the recipes you like and don't assume that you'll remember them simply because you make it often. Save everything you can because the thought you save might well be your own.

2. Make friends and keep in touch. I had a Johnson and Wales intern tell me once that all of the students were color coded. For example, the pastry students may wear a blue neckerchief while the savory students wear red. The savory and pastry students didn't socialize with each other, and it was easy to tell if someone what breaking the code because of the neckerchief color they wore. I didn't understand it because all of them were students in the same school and they all had culinary experiences in the kitchen. I encourage you to get to know your classmates. As you have seen in my story, most of my jobs were the result of other people recommending me when I was not even aware that a position was open. Your classmate can be your next boss, your next co-worker, or the person who opens the door or slams it shut in your face. Make friends and get their information. Social media is everywhere, so between Facebook, LinkedIn, Twitter, e-mails, text messaging and all of the other options that will be invented over time, there's no excuse for not keeping in touch.

3. Stay active in your local ACF Chapter. It is through your ACF Chapter that you meet more people, become more aware of policy/procedures, Robert's Rules of Orders, and a whole lot more. Your local Chapter grants you access to education, networking opportunities, job opportunities and did I say networking opportunities because that is really important. Learning opportunities, hands on skills/training. And, did I say networking already because that's just really important. Plus, it helps you stay in touch and connected with people in your community who are like-minded. It also allows you to teach other people what you've learned, to share your knowledge and pass it on which is what I'm doing. Somebody's taken time out to talk with you and to teach you. In turn, you should take the time to teach and show somebody else what you know. There's always something you can teach somebody. There's always somebody who wants to learn something. Stay connected with your community. People who are in the trenches with you appreciate and embrace that. You should as well. Always look out for the other person because it could be you that needs to be looked out for. Trust me, eventually it will be. We all need a break; make sure you're there to give somebody theirs.

4. *Always be open-minded and ready to receive.* Never close down, shut down, when you are in the process of learning something or being shown something. Too many times I have had an apprentice, an intern, extern, somebody who was still in school telling me how they did it, how to do something, that I was doing in my shop. Well, I, as the Executive Chef, am listening because there's always more than one way to skin a cat. I'm always good to listen, but when I, the Executive Chef, tell you why your idea is not going to work or why I prefer to do it the way we're doing, then you should listen. You should take the note, you should take heed, and you should write that down because, not to say that your idea will not work, it just will not work right now for me at this particular point and time. Maybe in another situation, another work environment, it would be great, you would have to do it that way.

So, it's not like you're being ignored, but also, when you're in somebody else's shop, or somebody else' kitchen, there's a chain of command and there's a decorum, there's rules that need to be followed and adhered to. So, if you have an idea, that's great, most chefs, I hope, are open-minded and they will listen. But then you, on the other hand, have to have the same respect that when they tell you it's this way, there's a reason why, you should expect that, acknowledge it, and do as requested. That is your job, that it why you're there, to produce and learn.

My hope is that by opening up and writing this, I can show someone that becoming an Executive Chef or Executive Pastry Chef is possible even when you come from the humblest beginnings. There are Chefs who are willing and waiting on you to step up and take control of your future. People are noticing and commenting on the plight of the minority chef. Culinary classes are filled with women, yet the leadership in our kitchen brigades does not reflect this. Are the women not getting the opportunity or are they just not taking it? You have to find your strength and courage to step out on your ability to succeed and lead. I was asked how one becomes a chef if you have never been one. Experience and awareness is the answer.

You have worked with cooks, sous chefs, Culinary Educators and Executive Chefs and you have experienced their management style. How they run their kitchens and delegated the work load. Was working for them a positive or negative experience? Did they earn your respect and trust and make you want to work more hours to help and learn? Mirror that! Imitation of a successful leader is admirable. If working for the same people make you nervous, feel left out of the planning and execution stages and or stunts your professional growth, remember these feelings and don't ever repeat this style of mismanagement. Why would you want to make anyone else feel that way?

By being aware and experiencing the work ethics of the kitchen you are in, you are in daily training for success if you are open to it. We all have to start somewhere, the key is to start! I went from apprentice to 1st pastry cook to Executive Pastry Chef. I experienced 2 Executive Chefs, 2 Executive Pastry Chefs, 2 Assistant Pastry Chefs, numerous sous chefs & Culinary Educators in the 6 years I lived in Dallas. I mirrored my leadership style after them all. I was able to capitalize on the examples and from knowing how I felt when experiencing The Snake or other's leadership styles. Take the lessons given and keep on stepping up to your highest potential.

It can happen if you plan the work and work the plan.

Don't believe me? Well, Here I Am.

Lavosh

4lbs 4oz All Purpose Flour
2oz Sugar
2oz Salt
1 t Cayenne Pepper
12oz Unsalted Butter
½ oz Compressed Yeast
16oz Milk
2 Cups Sesame Seeds or Poppy Seeds or Herbs

With dough hook attachment combine all the above except the seeds/ herbs.

Mix only to incorporate. Chill & rest dough on floured pan. Divide the cold dough into 6-8 pieces depending on the size of your baking pan. Coat the piece in the desired seeds/herbs.

On floured surface roll the seeded dough until it is wafer thin. If the dough is not rolled thin enough you will not have a crispy cracker. Place on sheet pan and cut the sheet into the desired pieces or leave whole and break them after baking.

Bake @ 375degrees for 10-14 minutes or until the cracker is lightly browned and crisp.

Serve or store air tight for 1 week.

Great for soups and salads as well as the cracker for the "Pate of the South" Pimento Cheese spread.

Black Eyed Pea Salad

2 Cans Black Eyed Peas –Rinsed & Drained
1 Each Bell Pepper-Red & Green Small Diced
1 Medium Red Onion-Small Diced
2 Cloves Garlic Pressed/Minced
1 Pinch Red Pepper Flakes
2T Freshly Chopped Cilantro
1 Bottle Balsamic Dressing

Combine all the above and let set in cooler for a minimum of 30 minutes to marinate.

Serve on Spinach Greens or Chopped Romaine.

This Festive Salad is perfect for the New Year's Day festivities and rituals. It satisfies the Black Eyed Pea requirement for the New Year very well and is a welcomed change to the usual fare. It is good year round and is a delicious way to incorporate beans/peas into your daily menu. Substitutions of white beans, kidney beans or lentils work very well with this recipe too.

Pureeing the beans first makes for a great "hummus" substitution served with pita or tortilla chips.

Chicken Satay with Peanut Dipping Sauce

10 Chicken Thighs -boneless/skinless cut into strips
1 T Ginger
1 T Garlic
12 oz Soy Sauce
2oz Sesame Oil
30 or more Wooded Skewers soaked in water

Combine the spices, soy and oil for the marinade. Add the chicken strips and refrigerate for 20 min minimum.

Thread the chicken onto the skewers and grill until internal temperature is 165F

1 cup Peanut Butter
1 cup Hoisin Sauce
8oz Pineapple Juice
6oz chopped Peanuts
3 each Green Onions sliced

Combine the peanut butter and Hoisin sauce. Add the pineapple juice until the desired consistency is reached for dipping sauce. You can microwave it to warm if desired.

Serve with grilled chicken satays with chopped peanuts and green onions sprinkled on top.

My friend and catering associate Dominique Milton inspired me with this recipe for the sauce. It is so good and so easy. I shared it with the guest of the Imara Magazine Empowerment Tour with great success. This is taking chicken to another level while keeping it simple and healthy so that it is easily duplicable.

Whole Wheat Pasta with Pesto Shrimp

1 lb Whole Wheat Pasta prepared according to package directions
2 lbs P&D Shrimp –Medium size
2 T Olive Oil
2 Cloves Garlic -Pressed or chopped
8oz Pesto
½ C White Wine
½ C Shredded Parmesan

Sauté Shrimp in oil until just pink in color. Add the garlic, pesto, and wine. Toss with cooked whole wheat pasta. Sprinkle parmesan on before service

** Chicken Strips, beef strips or pork loin strips can be substituted. The addition of veggies always will enhance this dish. Asparagus, broccoli, carrots, peas, spinach are a few to add.

Leftovers are great next day as a pasta salad.

Wheat Penne Pasta with Chicken & Red Pepper Sauce

1lb Whole Wheat Penne
1 lb Grilled Chicken Strips
16 oz Red Bell Peppers Roasted
3T Pesto
1 clove Garlic Roasted
1 Bulb Shallot Roasted
18 oz Veggie Stock
Salt & Black Pepper to taste
8oz Sundried Tomatoes- Rehydrated (optional)
5oz Shredded Parmesan Cheese

Prepare pasta according to package directions.

Simmer for 5 minutes Peppers, Garlic, Pesto, Shallots & Stock. Puree until smooth. Adjust with Salt & Pepper. Add tomatoes

Plate Chicken on top of pasta, add (Tomatoes &) Red Pepper Sauce. Top with cheese and serve.

Of course any pasta will be good with this recipe as well as other proteins. Fish, shrimp pork or beef go great with the red pepper sauce.

Mediterranean Style Lamb Chops

1 Rack of Lamb Chops Sliced or Whole
2T Garam Masala
1T Fresh Minced/Pressed Garlic
1tsp Fresh Rosemary Chopped
1tsp Cracked Black Pepper
3T Olive Oil

Combine oil and spices and massage into the flesh of the chops. Let marinate for 10-15 minutes before cooking.

Grilling on med high heat or broiling @ 375degrees to desired temperature of meat. Best results are for a medium rare to medium temperature so the juices and flavors of the meat are at their best.

Serve with Couscous, Quinoa or Brown Rice Pilaf and freshly prepared asparagus or broccoli.

I prepared these chops for a catered function a few years ago and my good friend Eliese Allen has been begging me for them ever since! It was her first time eating meat cooked medium rare to medium and she loved them. She couldn't believe how tender and juicy they were. Not tough and chewy like the other well done cuts of meat she had eaten before.

For more inspiration on this dish, go to my website www.chefkimberlybrockbrown.net for the You Tube video from the ABC "Low Country Live" Television show.

Fruit & Vegetable Curried Stew

1C Green Bell Peppers - Medium Diced
1C Medium Red Onion -Medium Diced
1lb Sweet Potatoes – Medium Diced
2 Cloves Garlic Chopped
6oz Peanut Butter
8oz Honey
1 Pinch Red Pepper Flakes
6oz Dried Apricots-Chopped
6oz Dried Cranberries
3T Curry
24oz Water
½ C Cilantro-Chopped for garnish
½ C Scallions-Chopped for garnish

In a large pot combine all ingredients over medium high heat to a boil. Reduce heat and simmer until the potatoes are tender. Add the cilantro and serve over brown rice or quinoa or couscous. Top with the sliced scallions before service.

I discovered this recipe in my Sodexo file and used it first at a community health event in North Charleston. I have modified the recipe to add more layers of flavors and colors and to eliminate the vegetables that did not stew well. This very flavorful dish will please the crowd and have them salivating with the smells of the peanut and curry permeating the air. When served with the quinoa, you have a completely balanced meal of protein, fruit, veggies and carbohydrates.

This stew freezes well for those days when you have more mouths to feed then time.

Sugar Dough

1lb 8oz Unsalted Butter
12oz Sugar
3 Eggs
1t Vanilla Extract
½ t Lemon Extract
2lb 4oz All Purpose Flour

Cream butter and sugar, combine the extracts and eggs and add. Scrape the bowl. Add the flour and mix only to incorporate. Chill dough before rolling.

This recipe is a pastry shop stock recipe meaning it is used for a variety of items. Tart shells and cookies are made from this basic recipe. Add ground nuts and more flavor for a very nutty cookie. Use this as a base for pastry and tortes. Of course any size tart shell is the main function of this recipe. The dough will freeze well for about a month if wrapped air-tight.

Florentine

Sugar dough crust par-baked with the sides, spread with thin layer of bake proof jam (Seedless Raspberry or Apricot) on a 12 X 18 inch parchment lined sheet pan.

4oz Heavy Cream
4oz Sugar
3oz Honey
4oz Unsalted Butter
1lb Sliced Almonds
Optional-Candied Fruit diced
Optional Semi-sweet Chocolate

Bring to a simmer the first 4 ingredients. Stir in the almonds and fruit. Remove from heat and spread on a cooled, blond baked sugar dough sheet layered with jam. Bake @ 350 degrees for 12 -15 minutes or until the almonds are golden brown. Cool completely and cut into desired sizes and shapes.

If desired melt the chocolate and dip the edge in it or drizzle the chocolate on top.

This classic cookie freezes well and is great for shipping to love ones far away during the holidays or whenever they are not near.

Pear Bread Pudding

12oz multigrain or wheat bread, cut into cubes
2T unsalted butter
1oz canola oil
3 large, firm yet ripe pears, peeled, halved, cored and thinly sliced
2 pinches Ginger
3 cups 1% low-fat Milk
2 Eggs, lightly beaten
3 T Light Brown Sugar-Divided
2 T Agave Syrup
2 t Vanilla extract
1 t grd Cinnamon
1/8 t grd Cloves

Directions

Preheat the oven to 350 F. Lightly coat a 9-inch square baking dish with cooking spray. Arrange the bread cubes in a single layer on a baking sheet. Bake until lightly toasted, about 5 minutes. Set aside.In a large, nonstick frying pan, melt the butter over medium heat until frothy. Stir in the canola oil. Add half of the pear slices to the pan and saute until evenly browned, about 10 minutes. Sprinkle a generous pinch of ginger onto the pears, then transfer them to a plate. Repeat with the remaining butter, oil, pears and ginger. Arrange half of the toasted bread cubes evenly in the bottom of the prepared baking dish. Top with half of the sauteed pears and then the remaining bread cubes.

In a large bowl, combine the milk, eggs, sugar, Agave, vanilla, cinnamon and cloves. Whisk until well blended. Pour the milk mixture over the bread and cover. Let stand for 20 minutes or until the bread absorbs the milk mixture. Arrange the remaining pears on top. Sprinkle with the remaining sugar.

Bake until a knife inserted into the center of the pudding comes out clean, 45 to 55 minutes. Enjoy!

This recipe is diabetic friendly yet good for anyone! High in fiber and flavor it is a filling and a fitting end to a meal. I served this to a group at the Tri-County Black Nurse's Health Symposium to help educate the public on how to eat good, nutritious, economical and easy to prepare food. Eating healthy should not be a burdensome chore that is frowned upon when it's time to prepare the meals. Giving people the tools and ideas on what to do with the foods on hand or are readily available is the key to a successful way of eating daily.

White Chocolate Bread Pudding

1 ½ lb Croissants –Diced
1 lb White Chocolate Couverture
1 lb Sugar & 1 cup reserved
12oz Yolks
1 Vanilla Bean split
26oz Heavy Cream
7oz Milk

Spray the baking vessel (cups, cake pan, ramekin) and dust with the reserved sugar.

Bring Liquids and vanilla bean to a simmer. Combine and mix well yolks & sugar.

Temper yolks and add. Whisk to incorporate. Add white chocolate and remove from heat. Stir to melt all of the chocolate. Add croissants and soak for 20-30 minutes. Fill baking vessel and bake in water bath @ 350 degrees until set.

Serve as desired in the baking cups or cool and slice to plate it.

This pudding will make you change your mind about not liking bread puddings. There is no calorie saving to be found here.

It is very rich and decadent yet simple enough for any occasion. It is good served cold or room temperature and is great served warm. This will also freeze well for future usage. Do not use cheap or imitation candy chocolate as you can really taste the difference.

Try this for your next holiday dessert and watch the accolades come rolling in. This pudding is sure to become the new family favorite.

Praline Cups

1lb 2oz Unsalted Butter
2lbs Sugar
1lb Light Corn Syrup
1lb Cake Flour
8oz Ground Almonds
8oz Sesame Seeds

Cream the butter and sugar. Add the remaining ingredients mix to incorporate. Chill dough. Scoop the chilled dough onto a parchment lined sheet pan.

If using a #32 scoop place no more than 6 on a sheet. Bake @350 degrees until they are golden brown. Remove from oven and let set for 15- 20 seconds before you invert each over a cup or bowl to mold it. The cup will cool and set into shape. Fill with your choice of cream, sorbet, fruits or mousse only when you are ready to serve as the moisture & humidity will make the cup loose its shape.

These crunchy cups filled with goodness are the perfect way to share your love. I added my love of South Carolina's "Low Country "by incorporating the Benne/Sesame seeds. They give the impression that you have struggled and triumphed all day in the kitchen to achieve such a masterful dessert. Whether making them as part of a combination dessert or as the featured attraction this sugar cup is sure to win hearts and rave reviews.

Sweet Potato Crisp

2 large Sweet Potatoes
4 large Eggs
1 cup Soy Milk
¼ tsp Nutmeg
1Tbs Cinnamon
1 Tbs Vanilla Extract
7 C Honey Bunches of Oat
½ C Melted Unsalted Butter

Cook the potatoes until tender in the microwave or oven. Remove skin and beat smooth with paddle attachment .

Combine the butter and cereal. Divide the mixture and set aside one half for the topping. The other half needs to be crushed for the crust.

On a parchment lined pan, evenly lay the crust. Par-bake to set it approximately 10 min.

Add to the smooth potatoes the eggs, milk, vanilla and spices. Scrape the bowl and mix to incorporate.

Pour the mixture evenly on to the cooled crust. Sprinkle the reserved cereal on the top.

Bake until the mixture has set. Check in about 16min. Remove from oven and cool.

Cut and serve.

Simple dessert utilizing breakfast cereal in the PM so that your money is not just tied up in breakfast fare. It gives the children and parents more bang for the buck by having a healthy and delicious dessert for lunch boxes or after school snacks. Served with ice cream it also makes a nice finish to the family meal.

Lemon & Blueberry Martini
with Candied Almond

2oz Lemon Sorbet
6 Blueberries
1 Jigger Vanilla Vodka
1 Jigger Blueberry Vodka
1C Ice
6oz Almonds
2oz Whites
3oz Sugar

Combine Almonds, sugar and whites. Spread on a silpat or parchment lined pan and bake until golden brown.

Set aside and cool.

In a shaker, combine the vodkas and half the berries. Muttle the berries and add the ice. Shake and pour through sieve over a scoop of sorbet in a martini glass. Garnish with remaining blueberries and Candied Almond.

Obviously I did not use those fresh picked blueberries to make this glass of deliciousness growing up. I am a fan of the lemon & blueberry combination and this satisfies my palette immensely. This festive adult libation is a great way to welcome in friends, family and holiday cheer! Or it can be a nice light finish to a filling meal.

I demonstrated this beverage at our 2012 ACF SE Regional Conference held in Winston-Salem, NC. It was one of 4 sessions given by AAC Fellows paired with a Junior ACF member to facilitate a mentoring and educational exchange. I hope this initiative continues as mentoring and giving back to our Junior student members is key to the success and growth of our industry.

2 sisters throwing it down! Aunts Marie & Lovia getting
spanked at the Bid table by Judy & Me! Christmas 1998

The McLeod-Bryant Family Circa 2003

Two of my favorite people Lee & President Obama

Three African American Female Executive Chefs!
Rare Indeed. Shacafrica, Dennie & me

My American Academy of Chefs Induction Day July 2003

Chef Kimberly at Grove Park Inn 1993

Sous Chef Brock & Me 2012

Cooking at the James Beard House February 1998

Chef of the Year 1999 Charleston Chapter ACF

Cousins Bianca Brown and Kyra Smith with Uncle Bill Mack

Eliese Allen, Aleta & Steve & me at the Moja
Luncheon honoring the Good Dr!

Mom, Lee Moultrie and me 2011

Here I am!